CLOSER

HOW TO BE A *STUDENT*
WHO MAKES *DISCIPLES*

ROBBY GALLATY

LifeWay Press®
Nashville, Tennessee

ISBN: 9781462748846
Item: 005794441

Dewey decimal classification: 239
Subject headings: RELIGION / CHRISTIAN MINISTRY / YOUTH

To order additional copies of this resource, write to LifeWay Resources Customer
Service; One LifeWay Plaza; Nashville, TN 37234-0113; fax 615.251.5933; phone toll free
800.458.2772; order online at www.lifeway.com; email orderentry@lifeway.com; or visit
the LifeWay Christian Store serving you.

Printed in the United States of America.

Student Ministry Publishing
LifeWay Resources
One LifeWay Plaza
Nashville, TN 37234

IN THIS

ABOUT THE *author*

ROBBY GALLATY is the Senior Pastor of Long Hollow Baptist Church in Hendersonville, TN. He was radically saved out of a life of drug addiction on November 12, 2002. In 2008, he founded Replicate Ministries to educate, equip, and empower men and women to be disciples who make disciple-makers (www.replicate.org). He is also the author of *Foundations: A 260-Day Bible Reading Plan for Busy Teens* (LifeWay, 2016), *Growing Up* (B&H Books, 2013), *Firmly Planted* (B&H Books, 2015), and *Rediscovering Discipleship* (Zondervan, 2015). He and his wife, Kandi, are intentional about investing in their two boys, Rig and Ryder.

A MESSAGE FROM *Robby*

You are about to embark on a journey that will change your life. I'm not saying that the words of this book are somehow magical. I'm saying that studying the Word of God, practicing spiritual disciplines, and being and making disciples transforms you. How can I say that? I'm speaking from personal experience.

Jesus expected His followers to make disciples, not converts or decisions. The word "disciple" means *student* or *learner*. Before we can embark on the task of making disciples, we must be a disciple first. *You can't expect from others what you aren't practicing yourself.* My prayer is that you wouldn't just read the words of this study, but apply what you learn. Put it into practice. Set aside time to study. Memorize, meditate, and incorporate what you learn into your daily life. Develop a plan of action. If you fail to plan, you can plan to fail.

Remember, you aren't just learning for yourself—the gospel came to you because it was heading to someone else. Every believer is either passing the baton to someone behind them or they are fumbling the handoff. It's my prayer for you that you run with passion as you draw closer to Christ.

R. Gallaty

ABOUT THIS STUDY

Jesus established the model of discipleship by forming and leading the first discipleship group—and it worked. The men who emerged from that group took the gospel to the world and ultimately laid down their lives for Christ.

In *Closer: How to Be a Student Who Makes Disciples,* Robby Gallaty presents a practical, easy-to-implement system to help students grow in their faith. This eight-session Bible study offers a manual for making disciples, addressing the what, why, where, and how of discipleship. Discipleship groups can create an atmosphere for fellowship, encouragement, and accountability—building an environment where God can work. D-Groups, as Gallaty calls them, can teach students how to grow in their relationship with God, how to defend their faith, and how to guide others in their relationship with God.

HOW TO USE

In this book, you will find content for eight weekly group sessions, daily personal devotions, and leader guide notes. Each session consists of a group guide followed by four days of homework. Included in the back of this study, there is also a leader guide with helpful hints and an outline of for each group session. As you close group time, encourage students to complete the personal devotions that follow the group sessions.

Once students have completed this study, they will have grown their faith exponentially and learned techniques for studying Scripture that will increase their own understanding of God's Word and prepare them for creating discipleship.

C.L.O.S.E.R.

TO JESUS

I THOUGHT THAT I HAD HIT ROCK BOTTOM when I stole $15,000 from my parents. I was only twenty-five years old, but I was already a drug dealer, hopelessly addicted to prescription medications, and was suddenly living with the police on my trail.

I hadn't started that way. I was born into a strict Roman Catholic family, and my parents sent me to Holy Cross High School, which was a Catholic boys' school in New Orleans. Even though it was a "religious" school, the extent of my worship was the hour or so I would sit in mass every Sunday. I'd do all of the rituals, say all of the sayings, and do my "Hail Mary's," but I'd leave each service entirely unchanged. I was completely unconcerned with what God wanted for me.

After high school, I ended up going to William Carey College, a small Baptist college in Mississippi, on a basketball scholarship. Imagine how out of place I was: a hulking New Orleans Catholic put in the middle of a Baptist college in Mississippi. I was suddenly the target of every evangelism class on campus!

While I was there, The Lord brought me a friend, Jeremy Brown, who cared enough about me to discuss what it really means to have a relationship with God. Jeremy's message was simple: If I would only cry out to God, He would forgive me of everything in my past.

But I didn't listen. I graduated from college and started a computer business with two friends. It looked promising. For six months, we poured everything we had into the company. But in the end, we just couldn't get it to take off. Exhausted, dejected, and broke, I needed something else.

Fortunately for me, I was a 6'6", 290-pound athlete who was fascinated with the world of mixed martial arts. I began training Brazilian Jiu-Jitsu and was soon hired as a bouncer in a nightclub in New Orleans. I felt like I was indestructible and finally on the right path: I had a job that was paying me to fight. But I couldn't have been more wrong.

When have you felt like everything in your life was going wrong?

What was happening?

How did it turn out?

On November 22, 1999, an eighteen-wheeler swerved across two lanes of traffic at sixty-five miles an hour and slammed my car into the guardrail. I suffered hernias and bulging discs in my back and was in horrific pain. The doctor I went to attempted to fix that pain with four very powerful, very addictive painkillers.

I'd never taken drugs before, but I soon found myself addicted to these painkillers. I was using a thirty-day supply of medicine in two weeks. I had to find another way to feed my addiction, and soon began using my business knowledge to import and sell illegal drugs so I could fuel my growing habit.

Although the business looked booming on the outside—and it was, because New Orleans is a famous hotbed for drug use—I was dying on the inside. Between 2000 and 2003, I lost eight friends to alcohol and drugs, and six more to prison. Soon, the police began monitoring me and those in my group. It shut the business down.

Soon, I found myself in a predicament: I had a $180-a-day drug addiction, but no income to support it. I couldn't pay the bills, so the gas, water, and electricity were cut off in my house. One day while visiting my father, I memorized his credit card number and began using it to buy things online to sell in pawn shops so that I could get money to pay my drug dealers. I stole $15,000 from him in three months.

My parents called me when they found out—and they were rightfully livid. They sent me to rehab and things seemed okay for a moment. But one day while lifting weights, I reinjured my back, had to get surgery, and was prescribed the same four drugs that had sent me down this path in the first place. Soon, I was back in rehab for another unsuccessful treatment.

Then something miraculous happened in my life. On November 12, 2002, I remembered what Jeremy Brown had told me four years before: that no matter what I had done, Christ loved me and was waiting for me to call out to Him. It was on the floor of my room, not at a church service or under a revival tent, that I surrendered my life to Him. I spent twenty-four hours locked in my room with nobody but Jesus Christ, and I emerged a completely changed man.

If you've surrendered your life to Christ, what were the circumstances?

What was your life like before you encountered Christ?

What was it like after?

Spend some time writing out a three-minute version of your personal testimony.

THE DIFFERENCE THAT MADE THE DIFFERENCE

I immediately knew that I was called to be a pastor, but my Catholic upbringing had not taught me how to read Scripture, memorize it, or pray. For several months, I wandered aimlessly in my Christian life, unable to proceed.

That is when I met David Platt at Edgewater Baptist Church in New Orleans. He invited me to meet weekly with him for Bible study, prayer, and accountability. We met every week for the next five months to discuss the glory of God, the lost nature of man, and the good news of Jesus Christ. I soon enrolled in seminary and we added more people to our weekly meetings. We met every Tuesday and Thursday morning at 6:30 for the next eighteen months.

What I learned with David is what we call Discipleship. It was a period of time in which we were intensely devoted to studying and memorizing Scripture, keeping one another accountable, and praying. But this is not something David invented; He got it straight from the life of Jesus.

The Bible records that Jesus ministered to three distinct groups of people: large groups, small groups, and one group of three. Jesus' large group ministry consisted of speaking to crowds (see the Sermon on the Mount, Matthew 5–7) and the 70 followers He sent out in Luke 10. These are all too large to be considered groups focused on discipleship.

Out of that large group, Jesus called twelve to be His closest followers (Mark 3:16-19; Luke 6:14-19). These are the most famous disciples in the Bible, because they followed Jesus closely for the three years He ministered on earth. This is the group He lived life with and spent the most time around.

Within that small group, He consistently took three of His disciples with Him for intensive times of equipping: Peter, James, and John. All three were fishermen and appear together five times in the Gospels—in Mark 1:29-31; Mark 5:37; Mark 9:2; Mark 13:3; and Matthew 26:37. This was His inner circle, the ones He lived most closely with, the ones He taught most directly and intimately. He lived out Solomon's wisdom from Ecclesiastes 4:9,12, which says, "Two are better than one... And if someone overpowers one person, two can resist him. A cord of three strands is not easily broken."

Has anyone ever taken the time to pour into you—whether it was for academic help, spiritual guidance, athletic training, etc.?

If so, how did their effort help you learn?

How did it make you feel knowing that they were pouring themselves out to help you?

If you developed your own "inner circle" of three or four people, who would you include? Why?

MULTIPLICATION, NOT ADDITION

The final instruction Jesus gave His disciples was to "Go, therefore, and make disciples of all nations, baptizing them in the name of the Father and of the Son and of the Holy Spirit, teaching them to observe everything I have commanded you" (Matt. 28:19-20). This is when we see His method of discipleship come full circle: when the one who was discipled turns into the one who disciples others. Everything they learned in their time of being discipled was not for them to keep to themselves, but for them to turn and teach someone else. We call this multiplication.

Imagine that a great evangelist could reach one person a day for an entire year. The first year, he'd reach 365 people, in the next year he'd reach another 365, totaling 730 people. That's a lot! In 16 years, he would have reached 5,840 people with the gospel.

Now imagine that one person disciples three other people. After a year, he would have reached only those three. But after that year, those three people find three people of their own to disciple. Then, the year after that, the people they disciple reach out and find three of their own. After one year, this disciple maker would have reached three, after the second he would have reached nine, then 27, then 81. After 16 years of this process, one man discipling three others would have reached 43,046,721 people!

Discipleship is slow because it is intentional. It is a time when you pour into someone's life for the purpose of helping them grow deeper in their faith—and to desire to pour into someone else's life in return. Over the next weeks, we are going to learn the principles that help someone grow closer to God so that they can be fully-devoted followers of Christ too. By practicing discipleship, we are going to actively make Jesus' final instruction our primary work: making disciples who will make disciples.

> *Even though we've only scratched the surface of discipleship, what are some benefits that you can see?*

> *What are some of the difficulties you could imagine?*

> *As a group, discuss ways you might overcome obstacles to discipleship.*

YOUR STORY IS GOD'S STORY

The distinguishing mark of a Christian's life is that there was a time when they first repented of their sins and placed their faith in Jesus Christ as their personal Lord and Savior. Every believer has one of these moments, and it's called a testimony. We should each be able to clearly communicate our testimony to others.

A common issue that comes up when sharing testimonies is that many of us don't know how to do it. That's okay. It doesn't have to be complicated. The easiest way to share is by breaking it down into three stages: 1) Describe who you were before Christ, 2) Explain the moment you came to know Christ, and 3) Tell how your life is different now. Let's take a look at each of these steps and what is helpful to include when sharing the story of how Jesus changed you. Then you can practice writing your testimony out by answering some of the questions provided.

1. WHO WERE YOU BEFORE CHRIST?

Ephesians 2:1-2 tells us, "You were dead in your trespasses and sins in which you previously lived according to the ways of this world." The first step in sharing a testimony is to describe yourself, like Paul did in his letter to the Ephesians, before you decided to follow Jesus.

What was your attitude like? Were you easily irritated by certain things or did you choose to stick with an "I couldn't care less" approach to difficulties?

Where did you place your hope?

2. HOW DID YOU COME TO KNOW CHRIST?

When the Philippian jailer asked Paul and Silas what he had to do to be saved, they responded with a simple answer in Acts 16:31: "Believe in the Lord Jesus and you will be saved." It doesn't matter where you've come from or what you've done; all that matters is that you simply turn from your former ways and accept the free gift that Jesus offers by believing in Him as the Son of God who died for our sins and rose again.

When did you first begin to understand Jesus' message of forgiveness and grace? How did you know your sin was separating you from a Holy God?

When did you confess that you were a sinner and needed Jesus to save you?

3. HOW ARE YOU DIFFERENT NOW?

In 2 Corinthians 5:17, Paul explains what happens when we put our faith in Christ: "If anyone is in Christ, he is a new creation; the old has passed away, and see, the new has come!" Once we are made new by Jesus after professing our faith in Him, something changes in our minds. We aren't perfect, but the focus of our lives switches from ourselves to Jesus.

How is who you are now different than who you were?

WHAT IS DISCIPLESHIP?

Do you know how many times *Christian* appears in the Bible? Only three times (Acts 11:26, Acts 26:28; 1 Peter 4:16). Many people believe *Christian* was actually a sort of insult. Those who despised Christ displayed their disgust for His followers by calling them, sarcastically, "little Christs." It probably wasn't until years later that *Christian* began to be used in a positive light.

On the other hand, the term disciple appears 269 times in the New Testament, with 238 of those occurring in the four Gospels. (The root word is used 281 times in the New Testament and 250 times in the Gospels alone.)

Why is this so important? The answer is because Christ did not come to make Christians; He came to make disciples. Immediately before leaving this world to return to heaven, He commanded us—His disciples—to carry on that work in His absence.

But before a person can make disciples, he or she must first be a disciple.

A disciple is, essentially, a learner who is set on growing and developing. We see disciples in our society all over the place: A tutor is assigned only to classes that he or she has already completed and mastered. Driving lessons are taught by an adult that has a driver's license and many years of experience driving. Someone training to be a doctor finishes medical school and must shadow an experienced physician. A disciple is simply someone who learns from a teacher!

We are going to learn a lot about the process of making disciples over the next eight weeks. But our focus is not going to be on driving lessons or medical school, it will be on the Word of God. As we seek to get shaped into the image of Christ, we will be learning directly from God through His Word.

What is the difference between being called a "Christian" and being a disciple, especially in today's culture?

What are your goals as you start this discipleship journey?

Take stock of your life for a moment. In what ways is your walk with the Lord strong? In what ways could it be improved?

WHAT IS A D-GROUP?

In Ecclesiastes 4:12, King Solomon wrote, "If someone overpowers one person, two can resist him. A cord of three strands is not easily broken."

As we embark on a journey of discipleship, we are going to keep this principle in mind: There is strength in numbers. This is just as true when walking down the street as it is in spiritual growth. When you have brothers or sisters standing by you and growing alongside you, all of your efforts will be multiplied and strengthened.

A Discipleship Group, or D-Group, is a group of three to five gender-exclusive (guys with guys, girls with girls) believers meeting together for the purpose of accountability, reading God's Word, and Scripture memorization. They help one another grow into the image of Christ.

Following are some important concepts when it comes to D-Groups:

Transparency: Things will come up in a D-Group that are personal and sometimes hard to share. But you will only get out of it what you put in. If you are willing to be open and honest with the people in your group, you will find that dealing with the struggles you face becomes much easier—you will be able to confront them head-on and will have the strength of your group to help you.

Confidentiality: As group members begin to share difficult things with you, it's important that they know they're sharing in confidence. Personal and difficult life experiences are hard to tell sometimes. Respecting one another's privacy will strengthen the bond that you share together.

Commitment: Each person's individual commitment level will affect the entire group. If one of your members is not as committed to growing consistently or to participating in the discussion or study as the rest of the group is, you will be dragged down together. Have you ever heard the saying, "A chain is only as strong as its weakest link"? The same is true here. Strive for commitment when embarking on a journey of discipleship with fellow believers.

How comfortable are you sharing things about yourself, even if they're not pretty or polished?

Is there a truth about you that you think would change the way people think about you? What is it?

If someone else had something they were nervous to share, what would you do to reassure them that they could share it safely with you?

TRAINING IN GODLINESS

Have you ever seen the Rocky movies? They're famous because they depict the hero, Rocky, facing opponents who are more experienced, stronger, or bigger than he is. Rocky's the underdog in every fight and has to overcome incredible odds to face off against the final opponent in the climax of the movies.

Some of the best scenes in those movies are the training montages. We see Rocky lifting weights, running drills, punching bags, and getting progressively better all in a matter of minutes. On the one hand, these scenes are good because they show the importance of training and improving, even if just slowly at first. However, they also do the viewer a disservice because they make intense training look easy.

As a disciple develops into a Christ-follower, he embarks on a lifetime of training. Unlike Rocky, however, we don't get a three-minute montage set to great music to zoom through. For us, spiritual training is a daily habit.

These are some spiritual disciplines that have helped believers grow closer to God for centuries.

Prayer (Communicate with God)

Meditation (Focusing on God)

Fasting (Relying on God)

Study (Learning about God)

Simplicity (Seeking God first)

Submission (Putting God's will first)

Solitude (Getting alone with God)

Service (Selflessly helping those around you)

Confession (Acknowledging sin before others)

Worship (Giving glory to God)

As we get tired or start to lose focus on our goal of becoming like Christ, these tools can help you redirect your attention back on what matters: God and His glory.

Which of these disciplines have you practiced before?

Which looks most appealing to you? Which looks the most frightening?

What are some ways you can focus on growing toward God daily?

How do you think that using spiritual disciplines could help you train for righteousness?

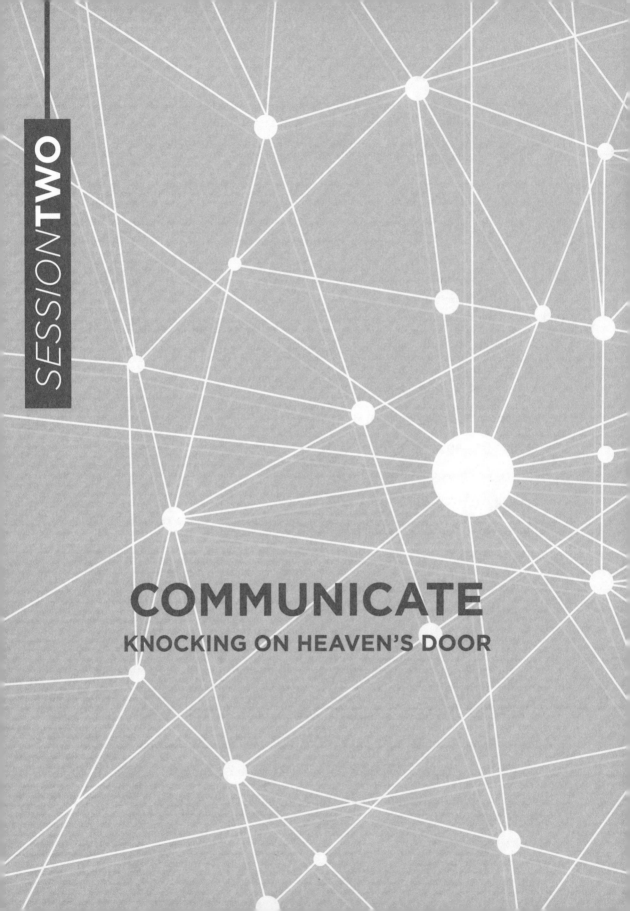

COMMUNICATE
KNOCKING ON HEAVEN'S DOOR

IMAGINE THIS SCENARIO: You walk into school on a Monday morning, still tired from the weekend. Your friends all seem to be dragging a little too, as you greet each other in the hallway before going to your first class. Math.

You take your seats and wait for the teacher to arrive, struggling to keep your eyes open. When he finally gets there, he is more energetic than usual and has a wry smile on his face. Your neighbor pokes you on the shoulder and asks, "What do you think his deal is?"

Your teacher soon says the two most dreaded words you could hear on a Monday morning: "Pop quiz!" Everyone in your class looks at each other with horror. One classmate puts her head down on her desk in defeat. Someone else sighs heavily. You look over to the friend who poked you and his head is bowed, eyes closed, lips moving feverishly.

That's when you realize that Ronald Reagan was right: As long as there are math tests, there will be prayer in schools.[1] This week, we are going to look at how Jesus taught His disciples to pray so that we're not like the friend in this scenario, treating God like He's a good-grades genie. It turns out that prayer is even more powerful than just a lamp you rub to magically learn material for a test you haven't studied for.

How would you rate your prayer life? Why?

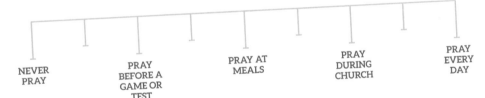

| NEVER PRAY | PRAY BEFORE A GAME OR TEST | PRAY AT MEALS | PRAY DURING CHURCH | PRAY EVERY DAY |

LEARNING FROM THE MASTER

Think about this: Scripture only records one instance of the disciples asking Jesus for specific instruction in something. They didn't ask for demon-casting lessons or how to be a healer; they didn't ask for tips on how to walk on water or lessons on what really happened at some event in the past. The only time that they asked Him for specific instruction in Scripture is recorded in Luke 11:1: "Lord, teach us to pray."

The disciples had come to understand that prayer was the source of all things. By observing His prayer life, they were eager to pray as He did. It felt real. It felt powerful. They wanted that. As we learn to pray, a great place to start is with prayer the way Jesus explained it.

1. "The Reagan Wit," *CBS News* [online], 20 July 2014, [accessed January 2017]. Available from the Internet: *http://www.cbsnews.com/news/the-reagan-wit/*.

If you look at the prayer recorded for us in Luke 11, you'll notice something extraordinary about it: It's only about 40 words long. This may have flabbergasted the disciples, because they were used to hearing the Pharisees praying loud, extravagant, wordy prayers in the streets to demonstrate their holiness. You, yourself, may be amazed when you hear someone eloquently expressing themselves out loud to the Father. Jesus' lesson was not in verbosity or eloquence, though; it was about the heart.

In His short Model Prayer, He taught His disciples as much in what He didn't say as in what He did. He taught them that prayer is not something learned in a classroom. There's not a list of magic words you must say to be heard by God; you practice prayer by doing it, not by learning about it.

> *Consider the disciples' request, "Lord, teach us to pray" in Luke 11:1. Using context, what prompted them to make this request?*

> *What are some ways your prayer life needs to change?*

A PATTERN TO FOLLOW

Most of the time, we recite this prayer as a part of worship or as the beginning of an important event. There is nothing wrong with quoting the Lord's Prayer, so long as it is not just a meaningless ritual. But it would be more efficient and beneficial to think of this prayer as an outline.

As you read through the prayer, notice the different parts:

- *Praise:* **Our Father in heaven**

- *Purpose:* **Your will be done, on earth as it is in heaven**

- *Provision:* **Give us our daily bread**

- *Pardon:* **Forgive us our sins (trespasses, debts, etc.)**

- *Protection:* **Lead us not into temptation, deliver us from evil**

- *Praise (again):* **Yours is the kingdom and the power and the glory forever.**

Jesus' prayer begins and ends with praise—it's bookended by what's important: our understanding that it is God alone who is worthy of our worship and our adoration. Using this prayer as a springboard, our own personal prayers can be modeled after it. Here is an example.

- *Praise:* "Father, heaven is Your throne and the earth is Your footstool. You have formed me with your own hands. You and You alone are worthy to be worshiped."

- *Purpose:* "All things work together for the good according to Your purpose. I am not my own, because you have bought me at a price. Guide me, direct me, and correct me in your ways. Help me say, 'Not my will, Lord, but Yours be done.'"

- *Provision:* "I will not worry about the things that I need. You're my Shepherd; therefore, everything I need, You supply because Your faithfulness is great."

- *Pardon:* "When I confess my sins to You, You're faithful and just to forgive me. You wash them away as far as the east is from the west. Reveal and forgive me for my sins against You and my brothers and sisters, so that I can make things right."

- *Protection:* "I have nothing to fear because You are with me. You never forsake me and You never leave me. Thank you for being my Rock and my Redeemer."

- *Praise (again):* "You alone are worthy to be praised and worshiped. Blessed be Your name. Amen."

  Rework the prayer from Luke 11 into your own words. Make it personal, highlighting relevant issues in your life.

PRAYER TIPS FROM THE SON OF GOD

Jesus not only offered us the Model Prayer, but He also gave us tips on how to create a lifestyle that revolves around it. From His Word, we can see six tips from the Son of God to strengthen our prayer life.

Pray Persistently

After sharing the Model Prayer, Jesus told His disciples, "Ask, and it will be given to you. Seek, and you will find. Knock, and the door will be opened to you" (Luke 11:9). Because we're reading in English, we lose a little bit of the impact from these words. More appropriately, Jesus told us to "keep on asking, keep on seeking, and keep on knocking."

Sadly, many of us don't pray this way. We can be random or irregular in our prayers. If you're ever tempted to be lazy or undisciplined in your prayer life, remember that Jesus promised us that if we keep seeking Him, we'll find Him.

Pray Privately

In Matthew 6:6, Jesus says, "When you pray, go into your room, shut the door, and pray to your Father who is in secret. And your Father who sees in secret will reward you." We live in a crowded, busy world, so it can feel difficult to find alone time with God. For that reason, we have to plan alone time with Him.

If you have trouble planning to pray, consider the "7Up" method: pray every morning for the next seven days for seven minutes first thing in the morning. Hopefully, you're thinking, "I can do that!" You can. But seven minutes may be longer than you initially think it is. That's okay; If you've never spent seven continuous minutes in prayer, expect it to be challenging at first. Don't give up. Press on, and soon you will find seven minutes turning to 10, then 20, then more.

Pray Corporately

We shouldn't only pray by ourselves, though. The biblical model of prayer always includes participatory, public prayer, too. Think how often the apostles and the early church met together to pray (Acts 2:42; 4:23-31). Like everything else, praying with others is a matter of priorities and commitment. If praying with others is important to you, and if you are committed to it, you'll make it happen. When praying with a partner or several people, ask for requests and then take turns praying for each other. It doesn't even have to be in person—nearly everyone has a cell phone or Skype.

Pray Precisely

Read from Luke 11:11-13. God is a loving father who delights in giving His children what they desire. This does not mean asking God for a sports car for your sweet sixteen. Remember, Jesus already modeled for us what prayer looks like. What He means is that while we are praying like He did, we should not be general or vague. Try asking God for these things and see what happens:

- "Lord, please help _____ come to know You."
- "Father, bless the missionaries my church has sent out."
- "Father, I know I sinned when _____. Please forgive me."

Pray specifically, because how else can you track God's answers to your prayers? Praying specifically is joining with God in the great work He accomplishes through prayer.

Pray Confidently

James tells us to "ask in faith, without doubting. For the doubter is like the surging sea, driven and tossed by the wind" (Jas. 1:6). We saw this modeled for us when Jesus came down from the Mount of Transfiguration and found His disciples failing miserably at casting a demon out of a possessed boy. The boy's father saw Jesus coming and petitioned to Him with a specific request (Matt. 17:15-16).

> *Do you expect God to move when you pray, or do you simply go through the motions of praying?*

Scripture is clear that God acts according to His will and purpose (Rom. 8:28), but at the same time He commands us to seek Him in prayer (Luke 11:9; Matt. 7:7). If you struggle with this, begin by asking God to simply move. Pray in faith, fully confident that He will answer according to His will and His time.

Pray Constantly

It is important to specifically make time to pray, just like it's important to seek out time to pray with others. But one of the shortest verses in the Bible teaches the true essence of prayer that the rest of it flows from: "Pray constantly" (1 Thess. 5:17).

This verse does not suggest that we should just retreat into a monastery where we can pray every moment we're awake; in fact, that is the opposite of what Jesus and the apostles modeled. To pray without ceasing means to begin your day with a connection to God, and then not to close it until you go to sleep. When you need direction, ask for it. When you need wisdom, request it. When you face temptation, plead for deliverance from it. Thank God immediately for every blessing and good thing in your day; praise Him constantly and tell Him you love Him. This is prayer without ceasing.

Adopting a life of prayer is not going to happen by accident, but it can be cultivated in anybody. Begin small and do it earnestly, then watch it grow into a lifestyle that is wholly, completely dependent on your communication with your Heavenly Father.

> *What changes need to be made in your schedule so that you can get up early to pray?*
>
> *What do you think praying without ceasing might look like in your life?*
>
> *Think of three people to pray for this week who might not know Jesus. Pray specifically that God would make a way for you to share the gospel with them.*

HOW BIG IS YOUR ROCK PILE?

Have you ever wondered how the Israelites could watch God part the Red Sea right before their eyes, and then turn around a week later and make idols out of gold? How could they have forgotten what God did for them so quickly?

Fortunately, God understands us better than we understand ourselves, and so He created a system to help us remember how He has worked in our lives.

The Israelites had been wandering in the desert for forty years when, one day, they approached the bank of the Jordan River. All that stood between them and the place they'd been headed for generations was a final obstacle: deep, rushing water. But when the priests' feet touched the water, the stream backed off—as if someone had turned a faucet off somewhere upstream.

Read Joshua 4:1-7 to see what God had them do next.

In a day without journals, computers, or iPads, God, through piles of rocks, imprinted His work on their minds. Every time they looked back across the Jordan and saw the rock piles sticking up above the rushing water, they would remember how God had brought them across it.

Throughout the Book of Joshua, God continued to work supernaturally and had the Israelites build stone memorials. He had them do it seven times, as a matter of fact. God wanted His people to remember His faithfulness.

We find ourselves praying for God to work in our lives, but how often do we look back and see where He's been faithful already? If we take time to stop along the way and keep a record of His faithfulness in our lives, we will be able to turn around in moments of darkness or doubt and see how He has already worked, and we will have our faith renewed.

One way to practically do this is to keep a prayer journal. Just as the Israelites marked God's faithfulness with stones, you can chart the things you have been praying for specifically. Then, when God answers your prayers or gives you aid, you can go back and record how He did it. It's your own, personal rock pile!

How have you seen God be faithful to you before?

How has He provided for you?

What is a situation you are asking Him for guidance about right now?

Even if it's just on a note on your phone, begin your prayer journal today.

PRAYING CONFIDENTLY

Have you ever found yourself praying for something and, at the same time, doubting if God will answer—or if He's even listening? Read what James wrote in his letter about this:

> But let him ask in faith without doubting. For the doubter is like the surging sea, driven and tossed by the wind. That person should not expect to receive anything from the Lord, being double-minded and unstable in all his ways (James 1:6-8).

When we pray, we pray to the God who created the universe. He is bigger, older, and more powerful than anything we could face. Furthermore, as John said in 1 John 5:14, "This is the confidence we have before him: If we ask anything according to His will, he hears us."

God desires to listen to His children, whether they are happy or sad, rejoicing or angry. He promises to hear you.

When you pray, do you expect God to move or do you simply go through the motions of praying?

God commands us to pray (Luke 11:9; Matt. 7:7). Why would He tell us to pray if it had no benefit at all?

In *Shadowlands,* a film about the life of C. S. Lewis, Anthony Hopkins, playing the role of Lewis, said this about prayer:

"I pray because I can't help myself. I pray because I'm helpless. I pray because the need flows out of me all the time—waking and sleeping. It doesn't change God—it changes me."[1]

We don't pray to get things, we pray because He told us to and because it brings us closer to Him.

When you pray, how do you pray? What kinds of things do you pray for?

How can prayer bring you closer to God?

How does the quote from Shadowlands *help you pray more confidently—knowing that God is listening to you?*

---

1. Anthony Hopkins, *Shadowlands,* directed by Richard Attenborough (1993; Burbank, CA: Savoy Pictures, 1999), DVD.

PRAYING SPECIFICALLY

In Day 1 of this week, I encouraged you to start a prayer journal. If you've used it even just once, you have a record of a specific prayer that you've prayed. Since we know that God hears His children when they pray, that means you have a record of a specific time that God heard you.

Look again at the passage from Luke 11:11-13 that we studied in the group session:

> *What father among you, if his son asks for a fish, will give him a snake instead of a fish? Or if he asks for an egg, will give him a scorpion? If you then, who are evil, know how to give good gifts to your children, how much more will the heavenly Father give the Holy Spirit to those who ask Him?*

This passage teaches us that God is a loving father who delights in giving His children what they need. But Matthew 6:8 tells us something even more remarkable—that God knows what we need even before we ask Him.

How comforting is that? Even if you can't formulate the words to express it, God knows. He knows because He made you. He stitched your heart together. He made the synapses in your brain that carry the electrical currents of thought, so He certainly knows the thoughts that they carry. We need to ask, of course (Jas. 4:2), but we can ask with confidence knowing that we're approaching Him with something He already knows.

Take two minutes and sit in silence, thinking back over your day and your week. Think about the relationships in your life, about the anxieties you have, about the things that are stressing you out, about the things that you're rejoicing over.

In your prayer journal, write out a prayer thanking God for what He's given you and asking for help where you need it.

How does knowing that God already knows the desires of your heart help you to take them to Him?

How can your prayer life change for the better from where it is right now?

WEAPONS OF MASS DISTRACTION

Allow me to be transparent for a moment. Sometimes I can feel pretty good about my spiritual life. I am a pastor. I pray every day, constantly. I pray in the morning. I pray with my sons before they go to bed at night. I have a prayer partner with whom I pray daily. I pray with others on numerous occasions. When I think back on it, I start feeling pretty confident.

Until I compare how much time I pray with how much time I spend doing other, completely pointless things. Watching television. Surfing the web. Checking Twitter.

This is one of the biggest traps we can fall into—feeling pretty good about praying for five straight minutes in the morning, just to log into Netflix and binge-watch a favorite show.

Think about this: Have you ever lost anything by missing the final episode of a reality show?

How about this: Have you ever actually gained anything by knowing the latest person voted off *Survivor* or *The Voice?*

Distractions come in the form of movies, shows, music, and sports, among other things. Can you tell me who won the World Series in 2010? In the realm of eternity, does it even matter?

Ephesians 5:16 commands us to make the best use of our time. So let's do an exercise for a moment. Just in your head, draw a vertical line. On the left, put all of the time you spend in prayer and reading God's Word in a given week. On the right, put all of the time you spend watching TV, playing video games, scrolling through Facebook and Instagram, or anything else of the sort.

Did it hurt a little bit to see that balance? It hurt me, for sure.

Sometimes we start to feel like God is distant, but if that scale is as out of balance as it has been for me, it might not be God who is distant. But know this: Just because you are distracted or that scale is out of balance, you are far from beyond hope. In Zechariah 1:3, God promises, "Return to me ... and I will return to you." What a merciful, gracious God we serve!

What is the number one thing distracting you from a close relationship with God?

What can you do to fix that?

LEARN

MINING FOR GOLD

"STUDY" CAN BE SUCH A TERRIFYING WORD FOR ANYBODY— especially a student. It usually means pouring back over notes that you hope are accurate, stressing out about what information might be on a test, and doing a good amount of staring off into space.

Some people approach studying the Bible this same way. They look at it as a huge book full of big names and ancient events and feel immediately swamped. Have you ever heard of the O.P.R.A. method of studying the Bible? See if you've ever done this:

O: **Open.** Open the Bible to a random place. It's God's Word, after all, so it should all be applicable!

P: **Point.** Since it's all God's Word, you should be safe reading whatever it is that you find. Close your eyes and point to a random spot on the page.

R: **Read.** Wherever your finger lands, that's what you read.

A: **Apply.** Think of some way to apply that truth to your life.

There was a man who wanted to study the Bible, but he had no way of knowing how to start, so he decided to resort to the O.P.R.A. method. He opened his Bible to a random spot and pointed. He landed on Matthew 27:5. "So he threw the silver pieces into the temple and departed. Then he went and hanged himself," it said. He shuddered at the thought and tried again.

He opened to another passage, this time Luke 10:37: "Go and do the same." His eyes got wide, but he figured he'd try one more time. He flipped to a third passage, this time John 13:27, which said "What you're doing, do quickly." He quickly shut the Bible and swore off it, because even the O.P.R.A. method didn't work and anything else seemed too difficult.

As Christians, our relationship with God and the Bible are inseparable. God has revealed Himself to us in His Word, apart from which we cannot know Him. You cannot be a true disciple of Christ apart from His Word. And fortunately, understanding what God's Word says is far from impossible.

Have you ever had a difficult time reading God's Word? What was difficult about it? Has that ever made you want to quit trying?

A LESSON FROM THE WORD

Many people could come up with all sorts of reasons why studying the Word is crucial, but they would all be man-imposed pieces of advice on something God, Himself, instructed. Look at the wisdom Paul gave the church in 1 Corinthians 2:12-14. Paul is careful to show something important here: It is not entirely up to us to understand what God says in His Word. We have a helper, the Holy Spirit, to give us instruction.

When we approach God's Word to understand what it says, we do so because God gave it to us, Himself. What He wants us to know has already been told to us, and we are not alone when learning what that is. Every genuine believer receives a wonderful gift at the time of salvation: the Holy Spirit coming and dwelling inside of us. He takes the things of Christ and reveals them to us (John 16:13-14). With His help, we can understand the Bibles for ourselves while relying on God's—not man's—wisdom.

This section in 1 Corinthians also tells us something else: that the Word of God is foolishness to unbelievers. It doesn't mean that God's Word suddenly becomes foolish, it simply means that, unaided by the Holy Spirit, God's truth makes no sense. Without the Holy Spirit to help us, we can fall into all kinds of traps when it comes to understanding Scripture.

Unfortunately, a great many people look at Scripture and twist it to make it say anything they want. Scripture has been used for years to justify all kinds of terrible things because the people using it didn't apply something called hermeneutics. That is a big word, but it simply means to explain or interpret.

A BIBLE STUDY LESSON FROM JESUS

Just after His resurrection, Jesus appeared to two people who were walking down the road and did something incredible with them: "Beginning with Moses and all the Prophets, he interpreted for them the things concerning himself in all the Scriptures" (Luke 24:27). Do you remember the word we learned, hermeneutics? It comes from the same word used in this verse, which is translated as "interpreted."

In essence, Jesus took these two disciples on a Spirit-guided journey through the Old Testament to reveal everything that it said about Him. We can do the same thing by focusing on something important: context. When we get a proper sense of where a verse fits in the bigger picture, we will be able to understand what it means. Here are few tips and then we'll do an exploration of a famous passage, just so you can see the process of studying the Bible—any verse at all—for yourself.

OBSERVATION: WHAT DOES THE TEXT SAY?

An easy way to study any text is to ask questions, and the first step is to simply observe what the text is saying. Begin by reading the passage several times, either out loud or to yourself. After familiarizing yourself with it, ask some basic observational questions:

Who is the author?
Who are the recipients?
Who are the main people?
What is happening in this text?
What are some key words?
What are the verses surrounding this verse?
What important comparisons or contrasts do you see?
When is this happening in history?
Where do these events take place?

You are like an investigator collecting evidence to construct a case. Study the scene, gather all of the evidence, and be careful not to overlook anything significant.

EXPLANATION: WHAT DOES THE TEXT MEAN?

After you have compiled your "evidence," you need to examine your findings. It's from your observations that scriptural truth will emerge. Just like in the first step, a great way to examine your findings is by asking questions. So take the things you noticed in the first step and ask questions like this:

What do the key terms mean?
How do the verses relate to each other?
How does this passage fit into the larger story of the book?
How does this passage point to or speak of Jesus?
What are the differences between the biblical audience and me?

As you study, you will find that each word in God's Word is bursting with meaning, and every principle will unfold in a compounding way the more you dive into it. But just gathering information and finding out what it means is not enough. This is God's Word, which He wants us to live out. So next we have to apply it.

APPLICATION: HOW DOES THE TEXT APPLY TO ME?

After arriving at some theological truths through observation and explanation, we get to the payoff for all of your hard work. When we apply the Bible, we focus God's truth upon our specific, life-related situations, helping us understand how to use what we have learned. We can't be satisfied by just gathering facts; we seek transformation. Just like in the previous two steps, we can ask questions about the truths that we have found to see how they apply to us.

Is there an application already in the text?
Is there a command or an exhortation for how we should live?
What does this biblical principle mean today?
What would the application of this verse look like in my life today?
How can this biblical principle help me grow in my relationship with God?

Remember, don't try to do this alone. Ask the Holy Spirit to help you, and open yourself to His instruction—and just like Jesus promised, He will. With the Spirit's help, you can understand God's Word and put it to work in your life.

PRACTICE

Something like this is too important to just leave at "theory." Let's see how to actually do this. Open your Bible to the most famous passage in all of Scripture, John 3:16, and let's study what it means.

> *For God loved the world in this way: He gave his one and only Son, so that everyone who believes in him will not perish but have eternal life.*

Observation

Let's see if we can answer some of the basic questions we learned to ask about a text in order to observe it. We'll get our answers from the immediate context of this verse, and also the larger context of the Book of John as a whole.

Author: John

Situation: A Pharisee named Nicodemus came to Jesus and began asking Him questions about being born again. **Key Words:** "God," "one and only Son," "believes," "perish," "life."

Surrounding Verses that may be important: Verses 14-15,17.

Explanation

How does this passage fit in with the Book of John as a whole?
John explicitly states his motive for writing his Gospel in John 20:30-31:

> *Jesus performed many other signs in the presence of his disciples that are not written in this book. But these are written so that you may believe Jesus is the Messiah, the Son of God, and that by believing you may have life in His name.*

This is directly connected to that verse. It even has some of the same keywords: "believe," "Son," "life."

How do the context verses relate to John 3:16? The two verses before this one are interesting, because they seem to reference something specific—a time when Moses lifted up a snake in the wilderness. Since Pharisees had intricate knowledge of the Old Testament, Jesus probably figured that Nicodemus would understand what the reference meant off the top of his head. If we want to understand what this passage is saying, we'd probably have to understand what Jesus referred to.

Your Bible may have references in it already pointing you in the right direction. Otherwise, you have hundreds of tools available to you on the Internet to help you find them. This one comes from Numbers 21:4-9. In that passage, the people had sinned greatly against God and He was punishing them with a plague of snakes. The snakes were biting and killing people left and right, and the people cried out for a way to be saved from them. God gave Moses some instructions: Make a bronze snake and put it on a pole, then raise that pole up. Everybody who looks on the snake on the pole would be rescued.

The connections to Jesus are endless! Two of them are obvious: Jesus would soon be raised up on a "pole" (a cross) and all those who truly look to Him would be saved. The situation is just like the situation in the Old Testament: We, God's creation, have sinned against Him and are sentenced to death because of it. We deserve this death, but God gave us a way out that we didn't deserve— someone to die in our place.

Put in this context, verses 16 and 17 shine brightly. The presence of Jesus is not a judgment on those who reject Him; it's salvation to those who accept Him! What we deserve is death; what we get through Him is eternal life.

Application
What does this principle mean today? It is still the best news imaginable. It's a personal invitation to be free from the eternal death that comes because of sin. It is applicable individually and for all people. They must ask themselves this question: Am I looking to Christ to save me, or am I perishing without Him?

Studying Scripture doesn't need to be intimidating. Let the Spirit guide you as you discover all that God has to say to you thorough His Word.

> *Do you already have a favorite Bible verse? With a partner, try applying this new method and discuss your new findings.*

I CAN DO ALL THINGS

This week in our devotions, we are going to practice the principle we went over in the main session: diving into God's Word. Following is a verse and some questions. First, read the passage, and then notice how we investigate the verse by asking questions about it. It may help to have a Bible near you in order to read more context if it's needed.

Philippians 4:10-13

> *I rejoiced in the Lord greatly because once again you renewed your care for me. You were, in fact, concerned about me but lacked the opportunity to show it. I don't say this out of need, for I have learned to be content in whatever circumstances I find myself. I know both how to make do with little, and I know how to make do with a lot. In any and all circumstances I have learned the secret of being content—whether well fed or hungry, whether in abundance or in need. I am able to do all things through him who strengthens me.*

Who is speaking in this verse? Paul

What do you think prompted him to write it? (What is the first sentence talking about?) It appears as though the church at Philippi helped Paul out in a time when he needed it. Maybe they sent him money, maybe they sent him provisions— whatever the case, they aided him.

What do you think "content" means? From the context, we can see that *content* here means that Paul is just fine no matter how bad the situation may seem. If he has nothing or is rich, he's okay with it, for instance.

What circumstances does he describe? Paul describes opposites: well-fed vs. hungry; in abundance vs. in need. He does this because pointing out the extremes includes everything in between.

What do you think "I am able to do all things through him who strengthens me" is referring to? Paul is clearly talking about how he is content no matter what situation he finds himself in because He knows his purpose and his goal—it's not about his comfort, but the advancement of the gospel.

Have you ever heard any of these verses before?

If so, has looking at the passage more closely changed your understanding of it at all? How?

IF YOU ASK, I'LL DO IT

As with yesterday's passage, it may help you to have a Bible handy in order to investigate these verses for yourself.

John 14:12-14

> Truly I tell you, the one who believes in me will also do the works that I do. And he will do even greater works than these, because I am going to the Father. Whatever you ask in my name, I will do it so that the Father may be glorified in the Son. If you ask me anything in my name, I will do it.

Who is speaking? Jesus

Who is he speaking to? The disciples in general, maybe Philip more specifically.

What request prompted this response? Philip told Him, "Show us the Father, and that's enough for us." Jesus asked them how they've missed it for so long since He's been there the whole time.

Why does Jesus say that they should ask in His name? To ask in Jesus' name means to ask according to the things that Jesus would want. If you go ask someone a question on behalf of your friend, you're not doing it because you are asking, but because you're asking in your friend's name. Jesus says the same of asking things of God: Don't do it for personal gain, but do it according to the way that Jesus would have done it.

What is the ultimate goal of what Jesus is talking about? (Do you see a "so that" in these verses?) The purpose is *so that* God will be glorified. This should be the motivation of our lives, so it should also be the motivation behind our requests.

What kinds of things should we ask for so that God gets the glory?

Do you think this passage could be taken the wrong way by people using it selfishly? Explain.

What are you doing to bring God glory? What can you begin doing today to ensure that He gets the glory?

JUDGE NOT

As before, have a copy of God's Word handy as we investigate what it tells us.

Matthew 7:1-5

> *Do not judge, so that you won't be judged. For you will be judged by the same standard with which you judge others, and you will be measured by the same measure you use. Why do you look at the splinter in your brother's eye but don't notice the beam of wood in your own eye? Or how can you say to your brother, 'Let me take the splinter out of your eye,' and look, there's a beam of wood in your own eye? Hypocrite! First take the beam of wood out of your eye, and then you will see clearly to take the splinter out of your brother's eye.*

Who is speaking? Jesus

Who is he speaking to? The crowd listening to the Sermon on the Mount

What do you think the difference between a "beam" and a "splinter" is in the context of this passage? A "beam" seems to be some big issue in your own life that you're ignoring. A "beam" in your eye would certainly stick out and cause you some discomfort! The splinter is something that is, by comparison, a much smaller deal than the beam.

Look up Matthew 7:20. How does that verse affect how you understand this passage? That verse says that we'll know people's hearts by the fruit—or actions—of their lives. So clearly this passage doesn't tell us not to judge anyone ever; it more appropriately tells us to judge rightly and fairly.

How do you see humility—thinking of others before yourself—in these verses? If you approach someone to show how you are somehow superior to them, that's an issue. It is a humbling thing to have to remove a "beam" from your life. It seems as though Jesus is saying that if we approach someone to remove a "splinter," it must be from a place of love, not meanness or self-righteousness.

> *How is addressing an issue humbly different from addressing an issue with arrogance?*

> *How can you address someone who is wrong with an attitude of humility?*

PLANS TO PROSPER YOU

The same advice applies here: It will be helpful to have a copy of the Word handy to investigate this verse.

Jeremiah 29:11

> *"For I know the plans I have for you"—this is the LORD's declaration—"plans for your well-being, not for disaster, to give you a future and a hope."*

Who is speaking here? These are the words of the Lord through Jeremiah

Who is the "you" in this verse? We have to look at this chapter, and the book, a bit more broadly to see the audience. Look at Jeremiah 29:4. This tells us God is speaking to "all the exiles I deported from Jerusalem to Babylon."

What is "well-being"? What is "disaster"? Well-being is essentially the opposite of "disaster"—ruin.

What "exile" is God referring to? The Babylonian exile was one of the most traumatic events in Israel's history. The superpower of the world at the time—Babylon—came and took away a great number of Israelites to be servants to the Babylonians. It was a dark time, a period of great turmoil for the Israelites, in which many people were probably asking where God was and what His plan was in the middle of all of the terrible things going on.

How do you think people may take this verse out of context? Many people have taken it as a personal promise to them from God—that even though they're suffering, their suffering will end soon and then their prosperity can begin.

What crucial bit of information comes in verse 10 that makes verse 11 kind of sour? Verse 11 is hopeful for the Israelites, but verse 10 must have felt like a blow—this promise wouldn't be fulfilled until 70 years were complete. None of the people hearing this promise would live to see it fulfilled! The nation of Israel—God's people—would make it out alive. But these individuals wouldn't.

How can we find hope in this verse, even if it wasn't meant for us? This is tricky, so I'll help you out. If you approach it from where Paul came from in Philippians 4:13, it starts to look pretty hopeful. Even if our situation seems dire, we can be content in the middle of it knowing that God is at work to bring His people redemption. We can cling to it for hope—not that God will take away all of our trouble, but that He will advance His gospel despite our situation.

OBEY
FOLLOW THE LEADER

I WANT YOU TO DRAW SOMETHING FOR ME. It's not a fancy drawing and doesn't require a lot of skill; it doesn't have to be big or pretty. In fact, it's really just a shape. In the space below, I want you to draw a triangle.

Now I'm going to have you write some words. At the top of the triangle, write the word **"Obey."**

Obedience is a simple term: It means hearing what someone has asked you to do and then doing it.

> *What is a rule you find it difficult to obey, but you still do? Why is it hard for you to obey this rule? Why do you do it anyway?*

Next, draw a down arrow toward the left side of the triangle, and then write **"Know"** by that corner.

Don't think of knowing facts; think of knowing someone. The more you know someone, the more you understand where they come from when they tell you different things.

> *Who is someone you know very well? How does knowing this person well affect how you interact with them?*

Finally, draw an arrow pointing right along the bottom of triangle and write the word **"Love"** by the right corner.

There are many kinds of love, but in general it is not something you feel, it's something you do. When you love somebody, it changes how you behave toward them!

> *What do you think love is? How does love affect how you treat someone?*

Complete the arrows going around your triangle by drawing one from **"Love"** to **"Obey."**

This triangle is now a representation of a growing relationship with God.

1) The more you obey God, the better you will know Him. You'll know where His heart lies, you'll know how He wants you to behave, you'll know how He feels about others—because you'll be doing the things He commands!

2) The more you know God, the more you'll love God. As you learn more about Him, there will be more of Him you can interact with and understand. As with human relationships, the deeper your knowledge of someone, the stronger your affection grows.

3) The more you love God, the more you'll want to obey Him. As your affection for God grows, you'll find yourself wanting to do more of what pleases Him. You'll find yourself making His wants your wants and then acting on them.

4) The process repeats over and over again.

> *Do you have a relationship in your life—a parent or a best friend, maybe—where you can see this triangle reflected?*

> *How do you think we make it so that we love and obey God above anything else in our lives?*

A WORD ON LOVE FROM THE DISCIPLE JESUS LOVED

Throughout his Gospel, John didn't call himself by name, but used the humble replacement "the disciple Jesus loved." He thought quite highly of the love of His Savior, so unsurprisingly he mentions it several times in his letters.

Look at what he says in 1 John 2:3-6.

In John's Gospel, he records Jesus saying, "If you love me, you will keep my commandments" (John 14:15). This passage in 1 John directly interacts with and expands on that simple, yet profound commandment. If we love Him, we'll do as He commanded.

LOVE FROM LOVE

One of the most famous superheroes of all time is Batman. In that story, there are two characters—Harley Quinn and the Joker—who are, at one point, "in love." We see how much Harley loves the Joker because she unquestioningly does all of his bidding and defends both his reputation and his life from the threat of the Batman.

However, that love is most definitely not returned to her. The Joker repeatedly threatens her with physical violence, shrugs her off, and verbally puts her down. This is not a picture of love.

A better picture of love comes from God: "We love because he first loved us" (1 John 4:19). So God's love for us is what motivates our love for Him.

God is not a disconnected, uncaring sky-dictator; He's the personal, all-good Creator of the universe. He has made love possible for us and has shown it to us more perfectly than we could ever hope to return.

> *How have you been shown love by your parents? By grandparents? A girlfriend or boyfriend? Your best friends?*
>
> *How do you best feel loved?*

Just because God has shown you love doesn't automatically mean that you're going to love Him back. You have to understand and know that love first.

If your love language is receiving small, thoughtful gifts, someone could show that love to you without you knowing it. Imagine waking up every day, only to find a small, unmarked, wrapped gift in the mail. You'd feel uplifted and loved, sure, but you wouldn't love the person who sent it because you don't know them.

Imagine receiving proof of someone else's love for you off and on over an extended period of time. You would feel uplifted; you may even love the sender back—but you wouldn't have any way of showing that love. When you finally found out who the sender was, you would be overwhelmed with gratitude not just for what they've done for you, but for the opportunity to express to them how much it means. You'd have a chance to love them back!

We've received immeasurable love from God, but in the same way as with our unknown gift-sender, until we know Him and understand the grace He's given us we won't feel motivated to love Him back.

Fortunately for us, Scripture records countless ways that God shows His love for us. Look up the following Scriptures and jot down some of the ways they prove how God has loved us:

Romans 5:8

John 3:16

Ephesians 2:4-5

Psalm 86:15

THE GOSPEL: THE ULTIMATE DISPLAY OF LOVE

The previous verses are merely snapshots of what is an unfathomably large thing: the love of God. In Christianity, we have a name for the love God has shown us. We call it the gospel.

"Gospel" is a word that means "good news." But we can't call it good news until we realize just how good it is. Understanding the gospel is absolutely central to Christianity.

GOD, THE CREATOR

You probably know how the Bible begins: "In the beginning, God created the heavens and the earth" (Gen. 1:1).

Have you ever created something? How did it turn out? How long did it take to get it to work the way you wanted it to?

Read Genesis 1:1 again. This tells us so many things about just who God is. Here are a few of them.

1) He's older than the universe. He had to have existed before the things He created did.

2) He's responsible for everything we see. Whether they are the stars in the sky or the bacteria under your fingernails, it was all created by Him.

3) It is to God we are accountable. If you made a toy—a yo-yo, perhaps— you would have every right to make sure it works the way you want it to work. You can adjust the gears and make sure it returns to you when you yank the string. In the same way, since God created everything, He has every right to expect us to work the way He designed us to work. This last point brings up a problem, though.

MAN, THE SINNER

God designed us for community with Him, but very soon after He made us, something happened.

Genesis 3 describes when something called sin entered the world that God created. Remember: Since God is our Creator, we are responsible to do what He created us to do. Since He made us for a relationship with Him, it means that we have to keep the relationship right.

But mankind did something else. When God gave Adam and Eve a commandment (Gen. 2:16-17), they decided that they were not going to heed that advice. The moment they disobeyed God's commandment, their action said something crucial: It said, "I know You gave us rules to follow, but we're not going to follow them. You may be the Creator, but we're going to go against what You said."

See, sin is not just something bad that you do; it's you usurping the power of the King of the Universe. Sin is when we put the desires of our hearts above God. It's when we treat someone or something else as more important than what God asked us to do.

Let me ask you this: If you created something but it just wasn't working the way it was supposed to, what right would you have to just entirely scrap it and start over? You'd have every right.

Greg Gilbert, in his book *What is the Gospel?,* said this about what sin means:

> "If we reduce sin to a mere breaking of relationship, rather than understanding it as the traitorous rebellion of a beloved subject against his good and righteous King, we will never understand why the death of God's Son was required to address it."[1]

This is why "the wages of sin is death" (Rom. 6:23). So far, this "good news" doesn't seem like such good news anymore, does it?

In your own words, what is the definition of sin?

CHRIST, THE SAVIOR

Our situation seems dire. Our rebellion against God is one that deserves death. But here's the thing: God loved us so much that He gave us a way out.

In the Old Testament, God made a provision for His people. He still required a payment for the sin that they lived in, but He allowed them to, with contrite hearts, sacrifice animals in their place. The problem with sacrificing animals is that humans sin all the time. In order to properly atone for their sin, they were having to sacrifice constantly. For thousands of years!

One day, God did something amazing. He sent part of the Trinity—His Son—to earth in order to pay that penalty once and for all.

Don't miss how amazing this is. He decided that seeing His Son beaten into an unrecognizable mess and crucified like a humiliated, common criminal was worth it in order to bring us back into right standing with Him. It's merciful because He's not making us pay something that we owe. It's grace because He did it even though we didn't deserve it. That is what is so amazing about grace.

In your own words, how do you know that Jesus loves you?

When we know who God is and what He has done for us, it will inspire us to love Him more deeply. When we love Him, we will hear Him tell us to obey Him, and we'll do it with glad, grateful hearts. The more we obey Him out of our love for Him, the more He will reveal Himself to us. Then the cycle of our knowing, loving, and obeying God will continue, more strongly than it did before.

FRIENDS OF GOD

Can you imagine the extent of a father's love for his son? He may care for strangers, he might have affection for his nephews and his cousins, but there is a special relationship between a father and his son.

During the final dinner they would share together, Jesus gave His disciples some pretty bad news: He was about to be betrayed by someone who was close to Him, and He would die. Soon. The next day, in fact. The disciples were understandably torn up about this—to the point that they were speechless. So Jesus took some time (several chapters' worth) to speak incredible encouragement to them. Look at one of the things He said to them in John 15:9-10:

> As the Father has loved me, I have also loved you. Remain in my love. If you keep my commands you will remain in my love, just as I have kept my Father's commands and remain in his love.

If a human father loves his son more than any other person, can you imagine how deeply God loved His Son? But still, Jesus told His disciples that He loved them that much, too. Even more encouragingly than that, He gave them the ticket to staying connected to Him, even when He was gone: keep my commands.

Sometimes we are going to encounter pieces of news that are terrible. We are going to question why things are happening. We will see situations and wonder what possible good could ever come of it.

In those situations, we have the ultimate fallback plan: Keep doing what Jesus told us to do, and we will keep the kind of connection between us that the Heavenly Father had with His Son.

In doing this, we're more than students. He says in verse 15, "I do not call you servants anymore...I have called you friends."

Times will get rough and situations will be out of our control, but we have the best security anybody could have: We can be called friends of God.

When was a time you felt like a situation was entirely out of your control?

How does it comfort you knowing that you are considered a friend of God?

STANDING ON THE PROMISES

We learned in the group session about the triangle that describes a growing relationship with the Lord:

The more we know God, the more we love Him. The more we love Him, the more we'll want to obey Him. The more we obey Him, the more He reveals Himself to us, and the better we'll know Him. It is a continuing process.

Well, as we love God enough to obey Him, He actually promises that He will shower us with benefits. Don't think of these benefits like money or cars or fame. Instead, let's look at places in His Word where we see the actual, literal benefits of a close, growing relationship with God:

- You will have assurance of your salvation (1 John 2:5).

- God's love will be perfected in you (1 John 2:5).

- You will be successful (Josh. 1:8).

- Your prayers will be answered (John 15:7).

- You will enjoy friendship with Christ (John 15:14).

- Your needs will be met (Matt. 6:33).

- God will direct your path in life (Prov. 3:5-6).

As we continue to know God by obeying Him, we'll keep the cycle of our relationship flowing, growing deeper and deeper into a walk with God.

This is such good news for us! It will be hard at times, but know that the benefits of persevering far outweigh the difficulty we will face. In fact, many of the benefits that God showers on us from close fellowship with Him will help keep us close to Him. For instance: The more sure we are of our salvation, the bolder we'll be to follow Him (which will cause Him to reveal more of Himself to us).

As you walk and find your steps getting weary, know that God's promises are sure footing. You can stand there and be replenished, because God's Word is perfect and always true.

What promise listed above speaks most strongly to you?

Can you search through Scripture and find more promises God gives to those who obey Him?

How does God want you to obey Him today?

WHAT LOVING GOD MEANS

During the Last Supper, Jesus gave His disciples a "new commandment," as He called it: "Just as I have loved you, you are also to love one another. By this everyone will know that you are my disciples, if you have love for one another" (John 13:34-35).

Even though He called it a new commandment, it was hardly something they'd never heard before. When Jesus was asked what the greatest commandment in the Old Testament was, He said "Love the Lord your God with all your heart, with all your soul, and with all your mind. This is the greatest and most important command. The second is like it: Love your neighbor as yourself" (Matt. 22:37-39). He connected two separate commands into one great command that can be summarized in one word: love.

When Jesus linked love for God and love for others, He did something amazing. He made it so that it's simply not possible to say that we love God if we don't love the people around us. John, the disciple Jesus loved, hammered this home in 2 John 1:6:

> This is love: that we walk according to his commands. This is the command as you have heard it from the beginning: that you walk in love.

In these verses we keep seeing the same words pop up over and over again: "love" and "command." We are commanded to love—and because we love God, we obey Him.

What this means for "love" is that the concept of it being only something we feel toward someone else is simply wrong. We could feel loving feelings toward another person, but it isn't love until we act it out. Jesus didn't command a feeling, He commanded an action.

Loving people can be hard. A lot of people make it hard to love them—but that's why Jesus made it a command, so we'd follow it even when it's hard. But He made sure to make an important distinction. We don't love out of compulsion or obligation, but because we love God.

Remember that today as you are around people who may seem unlovable. Look at them not as difficult projects, but as people you can shower love on because of your love for God.

Who is the most unlovable person in your life? What step can you take today toward loving that person?

What do you think it looks like to love people the way Jesus loves you?

THE COST OF FOLLOWING JESUS

One of the hardest passages of Scripture also tells us something absolutely crucial about what following Jesus actually entails. Read the account of what happened when several people came up to Jesus on the road and asked to follow Him:

> As they were traveling on the road someone said to him, "I will follow you wherever you go!"
>
> Jesus told him, "Foxes have dens, and birds of the sky have nests, but the Son of Man has no place to lay His head." Then he said to another, "Follow Me."
>
> "Lord," he said, "first let me go bury my father."
>
> But He told him, "Let the dead bury their own dead, but you go and spread the news of the kingdom of God."
>
> Another also said, "I will follow You, Lord, but first let me go and say good-bye to those at my house."
>
> But Jesus said to him, "No one who puts his hand to the plow and looks back is fit for the kingdom of God" (Luke 9:57-62).

Let's look at these three people. The first man's excitement was soon squashed when He found out that following Jesus was going to cost him his comfort. He may have assumed that this famous Rabbi traveled in style. Unfortunately, if you're looking for the posh choice, Jesus isn't going to be your first one.

The second man had what seemed like a reasonable request: Burying your father is a somber thing. The problem is that this man's father wasn't dead yet. What he was really asking was, "Let me have a little bit more time before I make up my mind." Following Jesus is not something you put off—even for something that's "good."

The last man seemed to have a reasonable request. He was going to be traveling around and so he wanted to say goodbye to those at his house. Jesus responded by using an agricultural metaphor. Have you ever seen rows of crops? They have to be very straight or else the entire field is thrown off. Jesus was saying that if a farmer started plowing and kept looking back, his lines would be crooked. As Christians, if we don't keep our eyes straight ahead and follow Jesus no matter the cost, we'll end up off course.

The cost of following Jesus will be high, but you have to ask yourself which is more important to you: your comfort or your obedience to the King of kings.

In what ways might following Jesus be dangerous or uncomfortable?

Is the cost worth it to you? Why or why not?

STORE
AN ETERNAL INVESTMENT

ONE OF MY FRIENDS IS THE TYPE OF PERSON who can walk out of a movie and, after only one viewing, quote almost the entire thing back to me. While not everyone can quote an entire movie, we're all a lot better at remembering it than we think! To prove it, take a couple of minutes to play a little game.

The rules are simple: You're just going to have a conversation. It can be about any topic or in response to any situation—that doesn't matter. The only twist is that you can only talk in either movie quotes or song lyrics. See how long you can keep it up before someone gets stumped.

How did you know the things you just quoted?

When have you ever been dealing with something that certain song lyrics or movie lines helped you get through?

It's hard to believe, but there are documented accounts of ultra-Orthodox Jews who committed the entire Babylonian Talmud (5,422 pages of text central to Judaism) to memory. To test this, someone could stick a pin into any of the 63 sections and they would be able to recite every word on every page of it.

In today's culture, these feats are almost unheard of. In the first century, however, memorization was critical. In an age when the only way to store and transmit information was to meticulously copy it by hand, people had to be able to quickly commit things to memory.

Specifically in the church, we consider memorizing Scripture to be something reserved for children in AWANA or a similar program. Some people may have a few verses memorized here and there, but few and far between are those who have entire sections of Scripture ready to be recalled.

Those who desire to be fully-devoted followers of Christ take Scriptural exportations like Colossians 3:16, "let the word of Christ dwell richly among you," seriously.

In Psalm 119:11, David says something simple that has incredibly profound effects on us: "I have treasured your word in my heart so that I may not sin against You."

HOW TO TREASURE A WORD

Some translations say, "hidden" instead of "treasured." The difference between those two words is a slight one—they both involve hiding something, but for different reasons.

What is something someone might hide?

What is something someone might treasure?

How do you think that "hiding" and "treasuring" are different?

David says that keeping God's Word inside of Him so that it takes root in his heart will do something crucial: It will provide stability in his life to keep him from sinning.

Now, of course, David didn't stop sinning altogether—nobody in history but Jesus has lived a life without sin—but the principle David is teaching here is important. When you make the things of God the number one priority in your life, obeying the commandments of God won't be a chore, but a joy!

These ancient Jewish people had very good memories, but they also had good methods for making memorization easier. We can actually see it in Scripture. Look at God's instructions to His people through Joshua:

> *This book of instruction must not depart from your mouth; you are to meditate on it day and night so that you may carefully observe everything written in it. For then you will prosper and succeed in whatever you do. (Joshua 1:8)*

It turns out that the secret to making God's Word dwell inside of you is to meditate on it day and night. When you hear "meditate," you may immediately think of a yoga class or someone sitting cross-legged in the park. Or you may be considering your own way of "meditating" as you study for tests—which ends in you asleep on your book every time. That's not at all what "meditate" means here.

When ancient Jews were mediating on Scripture, it was more like murmuring. It's a word that's related to "mutter," "ponder," or "study." The image that should come to mind is someone walking down the street not exactly talking to someone, but uttering something under his breath. But in this case, it's not just someone talking at random; it's someone reciting the Word of God.

Do you know how a cow eats? First, they bite and chew at grass. They swallow it and it goes into the first compartment in their stomach. After a little bit, the food comes back up to their mouth, where they chew it some more and swallow it again just for it to go to a different part of their stomach. They do this several times in a complete digestive cycle. The bit of food they chew up multiple times is called the "cud."

While this is sort of a gross image, it's the same kind of picture of someone murmuring, or meditating on, the Word of God. The idea would be that this person wakes up and takes in the Word through reading. Then, throughout the day, they keep bringing up what they read in their mind and "chewing" on it.

The key to the memorization process is repetition. As you begin memorizing, you'll only be able to take in small chunks at a time. That's okay—as you continue to exercise your memorization muscles, it eventually gets easier.

> *Is memorization easy or hard for you? Why do you think that is?*

Having the Word dwell inside of you enough to chew on it throughout your day would be difficult without memorization. Before the Word can become a part of your being, you must first implant it in your memory. Memorizing God's Word gives you the opportunity to contemplate it anytime and anywhere.

But strictly memorizing Scripture isn't what David meant when he said "I have treasured Your Word." People can memorize strings of numbers—that doesn't mean those numbers will change them.

Read Donald Whitney's illustration of the effect of memorizing the Word:

> You are the cup of hot water and the intake of Scripture is represented by the tea bag. Hearing God's Word is like one dip of the tea bag into the cup. Some of the tea's flavor is absorbed by the water, but not as much as would occur with a more thorough soaking of the bag ... In this analogy, reading, studying, and memorizing God's Word are represented by additional plunges of the tea bag into the cup. The more frequently the tea enters the water, the more effect it has.[1]

1. Donald Whitney, *Spiritual Disciplines for the Christian Life* (Colorado Springs, CO: NavPress, 1991), 21.

If you put the Word of God into you and recall it throughout your day so that you can "chew" on it, it's going to be on the forefront of your mind. Then, when you're presented with a situation that you would ordinarily react badly to, or if you're thrust into the path of temptation, you will have a piece of the Word of God you've been mulling over all day that will come to mind.

This is what David meant when he said that treasuring God's Word helps prevent him from sinning. We're human; we're going to fall short of the glory of God daily. But we can make an effort to prevent it by keeping God's commands at the forefront of our minds as often as possible.

THE BENEFITS ARE TREMENDOUS

As you continue to memorize and meditate on God's Word, you will find that the ways it benefits you are endless. Here are just a few ways that Scripture tells us it will benefit us:

1. **Meditation and memorization keep you from sin.**

   I have treasured your word in my heart so that I may not sin against you (Ps. 119:11).

2. **Meditation and memorization transform your thinking.**

   Do not be conformed to this age, but be transformed by the renewing of your mind, so that you may discern what is the good, pleasing, and perfect will of God (Rom. 12:2).

3. **Meditation and memorization equip you to share your testimony.**

   But in your hearts regard Christ the Lord as holy, ready at any time to give a defense to anyone who asks you for a reason for the hope that is in you (1 Pet. 3:15).

4. **Meditation and memorization provide direction for your life.**

   Your word is a lamp for my feet and a light on my path (Ps. 119:105).

5. Meditation and memorization produce spiritual growth.

And now I commit you to God and to the word of his grace, which is able to build you up and to give you an inheritance among all who are sanctified (Acts 20:32).

6. Meditation and memorization equip you to fight temptation.

Then the tempter approached him and said, "If you are the Son of God, tell these stones to become bread."

He answered, "It is written: Man must not live on bread alone but on every word that comes from the mouth of God" (Matt. 4:3-4).

These are just the beginning of what God's powerful Word will do when we invest the effort to treasure it in our hearts. Your list will grow even larger as you march on in the journey of your faith, encouraging you to memorize more and more of what God has said to us in His Word.

List some barriers that have prevented you from memorizing Scripture in the past.

What steps can you take in order to remove these barriers?

A WALK TO REMEMBER, PT. 1

The Christian life is often called a walk—which is actually a very good metaphor for how it works. One of the more extraordinary examples of seeing this walk played out in Scripture is in the first Psalm. Over the next four days, we will be looking at the first two verses under a magnifying glass to examine this truth, and in the process we will be committing the verses to memory.

> Blessed is the man
> who walks not in the counsel of the wicked (Psalm 1:1a ESV)

Have you ever walked on a treadmill? As the floor underneath your feet moves, you have to keep going forward in order to stay upright and not fall off the back. Even if you stop moving, the treadmill keeps on going—and it might just drag you with it!

Navigating life is like walking on that treadmill—you're going somewhere whether you're walking or standing still. As this Psalm begins, the psalmist actually starts painting a negative picture: telling you that it's good to avoid something.

The thing that we're avoiding here is the counsel of the wicked. Counsel is another word for advice or wisdom. If you were to go to court, you could get a counselor to advise you on how you should proceed. In school you have guidance counselors who help you navigate the tricky parts of education.

Those are examples of good counsel, though. The psalmist here says that we are to avoid the counsel of the wicked. If something is wicked, that speaks to the desires of the heart. They're corrupting influences that steer you away from the presence of God.

We are absolutely surrounded by these kinds of influences all the time. Whether it is certain peers at school or different magazines or media outlets telling you what is okay to do, the counsel of the wicked is rampant in today's world. If we are to follow God's path, we need to avoid these sources of worldly wisdom and stick to the one that will bring us to where God wants us to be: His Word.

How many corrupting influences can you think of in today's world?

What kind of bad advice do some of these influences give?

Why do you think is it so easy to get off track?

A WALK TO REMEMBER, PT. 2

The Psalmist continues the thought we began previously with a valuable piece of insight that has some deep implications. Let's follow his train of thought:

> Blessed is the man
>> who walks not in the counsel of the wicked,
> nor stands in the way of sinners (Psalm 1:1b ESV)

Notice first of all that there is a pattern that is starting to develop in the verbs that the psalmist uses. First, we saw that it's good to not walk in the counsel of the wicked. Now we're seeing that it's good not to stand in the way of sinners.

Imagine that you're walking around school and you see a group of boys standing in a huddle in the back corner of a secluded spot. They have their backs turned to you so you can't see what they're doing. What is your first reaction?

It may be that they're up to something completely innocent, but it's more probable that they're not. Not a lot has changed since this psalm was written—generally the ones standing still while the people around them are moving and being productive are up to no good.

A clump of people who are up to no good is fairly easy to spot. They don't walk up to you and try to get you to join in with them; they have to be approached, sought out. When the psalmist talks of the blessing of not standing in the way of sinners, it is also a reference to the blessing of not seeking out trouble.

But even more than that, watch the downward motion of the person in this "negative" side of the blessing: the man started out walking, but is now standing. His forward motion, signifying life, has stopped, and he is now settling and becoming complacent in his walk with the Lord.

Don't let your walk go stagnate; don't seek out sinners to stand with. As you keep your eyes focused on the Lord, keep walking in the direction He leads you, and you'll find it increasingly easier to pass those standing without joining in.

Have you ever seen someone whose "forward progress" with the Lord seemed to halt after they joined in with the wrong crowd?

What kinds of temptation hit you hardest? How can you walk in such a way as to avoid these temptations

A WALK TO REMEMBER, PT. 3

Yesterday we saw how a person who begins following the advice of wicked people will have his progress halted and may find himself standing around with the wrong crowd. Today this picture of wickedness is completed. Read the next part of verse 1:

> *Blessed is the man*
> *   who walks not in the counsel of the wicked,*
> *nor stands in the way of sinners,*
> *   nor sits in the seat of scoffers (Psalm 1:1 ESV)*

The psalmist has demonstrated with a word picture how walking in the advice of the wicked affects you: When you heed their wisdom, you stop moving forward; when you stop moving forward you end up squatting on the ground.

Have you ever seen a group of people who seem to live just to make fun of people? They may be the type that cracks rude jokes and laugh as they're walking down the hall at your school. Maybe they heckle other students from the back of class. The word "scoffers" refers to people making a mockery of someone or something. They are vocal and outright in their sin.

While this Psalm was probably not written to show a "downward spiral" from lesser to greater sins as one disregards the Word of God, we can certainly see that this kind of progression happens in everyday life. The second you start making allowances for little sins and tolerating the small things that you know you should oppose, it becomes easier to make bigger exceptions for even greater sins down the line.

Even if you have taken your seat among the scoffers, though, know this: It is never too late for you to stand and start walking again. It may be hard at first, because our muscles get used to sitting and our hearts get used to sinning. But Scripture calls you blessed if you don't walk how this man walked.

"Blessed" means more than just financial or physical prosperity. The expression "blessed is" in ancient Hebrew refers to the blessings of covenant life and the joy of living continually in the presence of God.

What is something that you can do daily to keep from getting derailed in your walk with God?

How can you keep your focus on Christ as you continue to walk?

A WALK TO REMEMBER, PT. 4

We've been walking through Psalm 1:1-2 slowly. As we finish up, we finally move past the path we're told to avoid, and the psalmist will give us the key to staying off of it. Now read all the way through Psalm 1:1-2.

> Blessed is the man
>   who walks not in the counsel of the wicked,
> nor stands in the way of sinners,
>   nor sits in the seat of scoffers;
> but his delight is in the law of the LORD,
>   and on his law he meditates day and night (Psalm 1:1-2 ESV).

After seeing a picture of what not to do, when we get instruction on what to do it should feel like a breath of fresh air. No longer are we looking for bananas on the sidewalks; we've been given a map that marks out all of the safe spots.

If someone is going to avoid the counsel of the wicked, the way of sinners, and the seat of scoffers, they have to have their focus set on the "law of the Lord." The word that the psalmist uses for "law" is Torah, the name that the Jews give the first five books of the Old Testament (for them, the only Testament). What it is intending to say is that the person who wishes to avoid verse 1 has only to do one thing: delight in the Lord's instruction.

It may seem strange to delight in instruction, but for the Jews, God's Law was life itself. It kept them on the "straight and narrow," if you will. It was proof that God loved them enough to keep them from harm. It was the boundary that defined all of the freedom that could be found in Him.

We delight in the Lord's instruction, too. When Jesus tells us how to have community with Him, we are grateful for it because that means we have a clear-cut path to making ourselves right. It is not enough to keep scanning our surroundings as we walk on life's journey so that we don't fall into a trap on the sidewalk; what we need to do is get God's Word inside of us and meditate on it day and night. When our heads are full of the Word, there won't be room to entertain the thoughts of the wicked. That is how being saturated with the Word of God will keep you from sin!

How committed are you to memorizing the Word of God?

Can you recite Psalm 1:1-2 by memory yet? If not, take a few minutes and try to memorize it. Remember the progression of the one who falls away: Walk—Stand—Sit. The mental picture will help you.

EVANGELIZE
SHOW AND TELL

IN THE NEXT FEW YEARS YOU WILL FIND that more and more people are going to ask you what you'd like to do. You'll have people asking you what colleges you'd like to apply to, what jobs you'd like to work, what you'd like to do as you start a family, and what the overall purpose of your life will be.

> *When you look at your life in the next ten years, what do you see yourself doing?*

> *What dreams or desires do you have right now? What are you doing to make them happen?*

One of the coolest things about being young is looking at all of the things ahead of you and seeing that it is truly a wide-open field. You have the potential to be anything, go anywhere, and do it with every ounce of who you are.

But that's not the same as saying that your purpose is limitless. If we talk about someone's purpose, we are referring to something bigger—an ultimate aim or goal. For instance, an airliner does a lot of things: it has compartments for storing luggage, trays of food to serve guests, seats that inflate into flotation devices, and all kinds of other things. But an airliner's purpose is to quickly transport people from one location to another.

For believers who have been transformed and made into new creations by Jesus, we have also been given a new purpose. No longer are we slaves to the passions and desires of our flesh, but we have been given a new direction that our life is to take. We find this direction in Matthew 28:18-20:

> *Jesus came near and said to them, "All authority has been given to me in heaven and on earth. Go, therefore, and make disciples of all nations, baptizing them in the name of the Father and of the Son and of the Holy Spirit, teaching them to observe everything I have commanded you. And remember, I am with you always, to the end of the age."*

> *How does Jesus' command affect the answer you gave to the previous questions about your dreams and desires?*

THE GREATEST COMMISSION

This passage is often called the "Great Commission." One of the most common uses of this word *commission* is in regard to warships. If a ship is commissioned, it gets sent out into active duty with its country's military forces. It is loaded with instruments and ammunition, a crew and a captain, and heads out into the sea to obey the orders of its commanding officers.

The commission that Jesus gave is similar to when the Navy commissions a warship. We go out into the field with the orders that our commanding officer gave us. Let's look at what that commission actually means.

GO

Interestingly, all four men who wrote Gospel accounts recorded His command to share the gospel with the nations. It wasn't just Matthew.

> *Go into all the world and preach the gospel to all creation (Mark 16:15).*

> *This is what is written: The Messiah would suffer and rise from the dead the third day, and repentance for forgiveness of sins would be proclaimed in his name to all the nations, beginning at Jerusalem. You are witnesses of these things (Luke 24:46-48).*

> *Jesus said to them again, "Peace to you. As the Father has sent me, I also send you" (John 20:21).*

While these books end with the command to go and proclaim the good news, the book of Acts begins with it.

> *But you will receive power when the Holy Spirit has come on you, and you will be my witnesses in Jerusalem, in all Judea and Samaria, and to the ends of the earth (Acts 1:8).*

The fact that each Gospel account and Acts record the same command—to go—should tell us something about how specific the purpose of a Christian's life is. We are to take the gospel to the nations.

But this doesn't mean that every single one of us should get on a plane and fly to the corners of the world. Certainly some of us will be called to do that, but the "Go" recorded in Matthew means, more accurately "as you go."

As you go to college, make disciples.

As you go about your day, make disciples.

As you experience hardship and have bad days, make disciples.

Even though we will do many individual things, the overall purpose of what we do has changed: We are to tell people the good news of Jesus and make disciples no matter where we find ourselves.

> *Describe your daily routine. What things do you do? What people do you interact with?*

> *How can you apply the mentality of sharing the gospel "as you go" in these things and with these people?*

MAKE DISCIPLES

The distinction between evangelism and making disciples is not as big as people would believe it is; they simply describe different points on the process of making a fully-formed follower of Christ. They are two oars attached to the same boat. With only one oar in the water, a boat will simply go in circles.

Think about the distinction this way: The gospel is received through evangelism and lived out through discipleship. If we share the gospel but don't usher people into discipleship, they won't have an avenue for growing in or strengthening their faith. If we aren't sharing the gospel, there won't be people ready to be discipled.

But how difficult would it be to make disciples of the nations if we weren't first telling them about the good news of Jesus? For this reason, when each of the authors of the gospels recorded Jesus sending the disciples out into the world, they each used different words: They were each emphasizing different parts of the same thing, our calling as followers of Jesus.

> *In your own words, how do discipleship and evangelism work together to help someone grow closer to Christ?*

> *Have you ever shared the gospel with someone? How did you do it?*

> *See if you can write out in just a few sentences how you might share the good news of Jesus.*

TEACHING THEM TO OBEY

Jesus didn't expect His disciples to free-wheel their way through discipling the nations. He made it clear what they were to teach: They were to do with others what He did with them.

Could there be anything more simple than that? They simply replicated what Jesus did with them in someone else. This shows two aspects of discipleship:

1) The only qualification that the disciples needed was the fact that they had been discipled by Jesus.

2) Disciples will make disciples that look like they do.

Jesus taught His disciples, then they taught their disciples like Jesus taught them. Then their disciples repeated the same! It is a trail that we can literally trace all the way to today, where Christians are still sharing the gospel and making disciples who make disciples.

Is it easier for you to learn something by seeing a list of instructions on a page or by having someone walk you through it? Why?

What would you feel comfortable teaching someone else? How would you do it?

THE PROPER PERSPECTIVE

When John the Baptist was preparing the way for Jesus, he said something peculiar: "Repent, because the kingdom of heaven has come near!" (Matt. 3:2).

Have you ever been to visit another country or a city that wasn't much like the place where you're from? When you are walking through another place that isn't your home, you look at people differently. You follow the rules, but you don't feel the same kind of connection to that place the people who live there do.

Contrary to what a lot of people believe, the "kingdom of heaven" isn't just a place we go when we die—it's something that you enter the moment you become a child of God. When you become the citizen of God's kingdom, you are like a foreigner passing through a city you're not from.

Paul explained that we are out of place on earth because we are citizens of the kingdom of God in Philippians 3:19-20. We get our meaning, our satisfaction, and our calling from something far greater and far better than the world we live in.

When Jesus sent His disciples out on that great mission in Matthew 28, He did something better than just give them an assignment: He told them what their purpose in this world is. So many walk around not knowing where they fit in or what they are supposed to be doing. If you are a child of God, that is something that you don't need to lose sleep over—because you do know your purpose. Jesus laid it out for us. As we live, we are to make disciples. Our lives become about spreading the good news!

Have you or someone you know ever struggled with knowing your purpose?

How does seeing yourself as a citizen of heaven change how you look at your surroundings?

How can you live as a citizen of heaven among your friends and neighbors?

THE CALL TO ACTION

Our job as Christians is twofold:

1) Obey Jesus' commands.

2) Give God glory in all things.

As we go out sharing the good news about Jesus, we have to remember what our role is: *telling people.* It is not our job to change hearts. Somehow over the years, people have begun measuring the success of our gospel sharing in "how many people get saved." Success in evangelism is in the sharing, not the saving. Only God can save, but He commands us to share. Paul made this crystal clear to the church at Corinth (1 Cor. 3:4-7).

But as we share, let's not forget the real reason that we're sharing—it's not to check a spiritual box or to make ourselves feel good, it's to bring glory to God. Nothing proclaims God's glory greater than His love for sinful people. The focus of our evangelism is not the lost; it is God and His glory. We tell people about Jesus because He is worthy of all their worship. If you say that you love God and you love bringing Him glory, then you should be talking about Him everywhere you go.

Do your friends and family know about your relationship with Jesus?

Who in your life needs you to show and tell the gospel to them?

List three friends, family members, or acquaintances who are unsaved. Pray for God to open their hearts, and pray for an opportunity to share the gospel with them.

SHARING THE GOSPEL THROUGH RELATIONSHIPS

We live in a world that desperately needs to see the love of the Savior. Fortunately, He gave us the method by which everyone can hear it: us. It is our job as believers to proclaim the good news that we've found wherever we can.

But gospel presentations are tricky to do, especially in a world that sees everything as a sales pitch. It's easy to turn people into projects, even if just in our heads, so one of the most effective ways to communicate the gospel is to establish genuine relationships with people.

Nobody wants to have a friend that is always trying to pitch something. One of our deepest desires as humans is to be heard, so start there. When you are cultivating a friendship with someone, be sure to listen first, and listen long. You want your relationship to be comfortable and genuine, so take the time to listen to their story and get to know the person that they are.

Then, when you get the chance to share your story, make sure to include the transformation that came through Jesus. It doesn't have to be heavy-handed or cheesy, it just has to be real. Jesus saved you—you may not be able to explain it, but you know that it happened. You used to be something, and now you're not!

It's hard to be burdened for our lost friends, because we tend to want them to just get it right now. The absolute best thing you can do for them is pray for them.

1) Pray that they will want to know God.

2) Pray that they'll encounter Jesus through His Word

3) Pray that God will draw them to Himself.

4) Pray that the Holy Spirit will work on their hearts.

5) Pray that God will send you an opening to share Christ with them.

6) Pray that they believe in and confess Christ as Savior and Lord.

In your prayer journal, write the names of four lost friends in your life that you will commit to praying for every day this week.

Spend a few minutes right now beginning the process of praying for them. If you want to, begin by praying for the six things listed above. Remember, pray specifically, because God hears when His children pray to Him.

WHAT IS THE GOSPEL?

In Session 4 we learned what the gospel is. But when we go to share the gospel, it's nice to see it written out for us in the pages of Scripture so that we can easily point to it if someone asks. One of the easiest presentations of it is found in 1 Corinthians 15:1-8. Read that passage here and then answer some questions about it that will help your understanding.

> Now I want to make clear for you, brothers and sisters, the gospel I preached to you, which you received, on which you have taken your stand and by which you are being saved, if you hold to the message I preached to you—unless you believed in vain.
>
> For I passed on to you as most important what I also received:
>
> that Christ died for our sins according to the Scriptures,
>
> that he was buried,
>
> that he was raised on the third day according to the Scriptures,
>
> and that he appeared to Cephas, then to the Twelve.
>
> Then he appeared to over five hundred brothers and sisters at one time; most of them are still alive, but some have fallen asleep.
>
> Then he appeared to James, then to all the apostles.
>
> Last of all, as to one born at the wrong time, he also appeared to me.

Why do you think Paul clarified that Christ's death was "in accordance with the Scriptures"?

Explain in your own words why Christ had to die to cover our sins.

Why did Paul point out that, at the time of his writing, most of the people Christ appeared to after His death were still alive?

Why is the resurrection so important?

How has the gospel transformed your life?

LIVING BY FAITH

There were few people more articulate at expressing the things of God than Paul. Look at what he says about the gospel in Romans 1:16-17, and then let's notice what it means for us as we live out lives that share it:

> For I am not ashamed of the gospel, because it is the power of God for salvation to everyone who believes, first to the Jew, and also to the Greek. For in it the righteousness of God is revealed from faith to faith, just as it is written: The righteous will live by faith.

What are some reasons people don't share the gospel? What are they afraid of?

Too many times, people are timid about how the gospel will be received by the people they're sharing it with. Maybe they're scared of being called crazy. More likely, they might be nervous that they will be asked a question they don't know the answer to and will end up looking foolish.

These are all natural feelings, but that doesn't make them right. When Paul talked about sharing the gospel, he didn't mention once that he was nervous about it. In fact, he said the opposite: he's not ashamed of it. The only time that Paul says the word "I" in this passage is at the beginning—the rest is about what God has done.

One of the hardest things for us to learn how to do is remove ourselves from a gospel presentation. As much as we hate admitting it, the gospel is not meant only for us. Instead, it came to us because it was headed for someone else.

There is actually a lot of freedom in knowing that it's not all about us. We aren't the ones who did any of the work on the cross, we aren't the ones who can save anyone, and we aren't the ones responsible for changing people's hearts—our only task when it comes to sharing the gospel is putting it out there.

If someone rejects the gospel that you proclaim, hear this, they are not rejecting you—because it isn't your message in the first place. The only message you have is "this is the news I heard about Jesus, and this is how it changed my life." If there's one evidence that no person on earth can argue with or discredit, it's the power of a changed life.

Remember what Christ has done in and for you, and proclaim His gospel boldly.

What is the hardest part about sharing the gospel for you?

How can you pray specifically that God will prepare you to bring His good news to anyone who will listen?

YOUR TESTIMONY

In the first week of this study, you thought about your testimony and how Jesus changed your life. But that was five sessions back—we've covered a lot of ground in that time. If you're like me, you've changed a lot over this period of time.

Today we're going to do two things: look at a passage of Scripture that explains what Christ did on the cross, and then use that to revisit the testimony you wrote at the start of this study.

Read Ephesians 2:1-5:

> *And you were dead in your trespasses and sins in which you previously lived according to the ways of this world, according to the ruler of the power of the air, the spirit now working in the disobedient. We too all previously lived among them in our fleshly desires, carrying out the inclinations of our flesh and thoughts, and we were by nature children under wrath as the others were also. But God, who is rich in mercy, because of his great love that he had for us, made us alive with Christ even though we were dead in trespasses. You are saved by grace!*

Take a look at some of the key words and phrases Paul used in this passage.

Dead in your trespasses and sins
According to the ways of the world
Disobedient
Carrying out the inclinations of our flesh
Children under wrath
But God
Rich in mercy
His great love that He had for us
Made us alive
Christ
Saved by grace

Does your story fit that kind of arc? How were you dead in your sins? Did you deserve what Jesus did for you on the cross? What was the outcome of His work on the cross? When did you come to realize this? How does that affect you today?

> *Spend five to ten minutes writing out a fuller version of your individual God story and then read over it several times. Thank God for what He's done in your life, and then pray for an opportunity to share it with someone this week.*

RENEW

H.E.A.R.ing from God

IN MY HOUSE GROWING UP, one of the quickest ways for me to find my way into the doghouse was for my mom to tell me something and then roll my eyes at her.

Here is another way I would find myself in trouble. I'd be sitting down and my mom would come tell me to clean my room. I would motion "I got it!" and she'd walk away. Some time would pass and she'd come back to find me in the exact same position, my room still a disaster. She'd say something to the tune of, "Didn't you hear me? I told you to clean your room!"

The thing is, I'd taken in the words that she said and understood them, but I hadn't really heard her. I didn't act on it. I'd done the first part, but I hadn't followed through.

If we go about reading the Bible just so that we bring knowledge about it or about God into our heads, we're only getting half of the picture. What is far more important is that we listen to what God says in such a way that it gets deep inside of us. We need to learn how to get into the Word until the Word gets into us.

What kind of environment do you learn the best in? Do you need a pristine, clutter-free workspace? Do you thrive in the middle of tornado-like chaos? Does it need to be silent or do you work best with a lot of distractions to tune out?

Try writing a defense of your "ideal learning environment" so that you can convince someone who thinks differently that your option is better.

When the Word dwells richly inside of us, we will see that it not only nourishes us spiritually, but equips us for all of the work God has for us to do.

WHY SHOULD I READ THE BIBLE?

If the Word is going to transform our lives, we first need to get it into us. An episode of Jesus' life shows why we need God's Word on a daily basis. Right after He was baptized, Jesus was put into a period of intense temptation. You can read about it in Matthew 4.

What made His experience unique is that 1) It was Satan, himself, tempting Him, and 2) The temptation was to do far more powerful things than you or I are capable of doing. But each time Satan tempted Him, Jesus responded not with reason or with anger, but with the Word of God.

When Satan tempted Jesus through His physical hunger, Jesus responded by referencing a miraculous event for the Israelites. They were in the desert without food or water and were forced to rely on God to physically sustain them during the day. After they complained to Moses about it, God revealed what He was going to do. He told Moses,

> *"I am going to rain bread from heaven for you. The people are to go out each day and gather enough for that day. This way I will test them to see whether or not they will follow my instructions. On the sixth day, when they prepare what they bring in, it will be twice as much as they gather on other days" (Ex. 16:4-5).*

This passage shows us two important principles:

1) Each individual had to personally make time to gather enough food for the day and then put the energy and effort into collecting it.

2) The bread they gathered was only good for that day—the next day, they would have to do it all over again.

Every Jew knew the story of the manna (bread) that came from heaven. So when Jesus was tempted to turn stones to bread, He connected the manna with the Word of God. How is the Word of God like bread?

- As spiritual beings, we need more than physical nourishment (bread) to survive. We need the Word of God.

- God's Word is to us spiritually what the manna was to the ancient Jews: life-sustaining nourishment.

- Just as the Jews had to make the time and effort to gather manna, we must set aside time every day to be spiritually nourished.

- Just as the Jews had to gather manna every day, we must read the Bible every day. What we read today is not sufficient for tomorrow.

> *Take a look back at the past month of your life. What is your Bible reading habit like? Where are some areas it could be improved?*

CONFESSIONS OF A BORED BIBLE READER

When I was finishing my seminary degree, I had to fly back and forth to school once a week for class. On every trip, I asked the people sitting next to me the same question: "Why do you think people are not reading the Bible? More importantly, why are you not reading the Bible?" The answers ranged from "I don't have enough time" to "It's just an old book," but the most common answer was, "The Bible just doesn't speak to me."

Asking this question and hearing the answers made me question my own quiet time. After I looked at it honestly, I realized that my own Bible reading had become routine and mundane. I tried everything I could think of to "spice it up," but nothing worked. After some prayer, I realized that my problem was not with the reading plan, but with me. I acknowledged that I was not approaching God's Word to hear from it; I was simply trying to read from it.

What I needed was not a fresh plan, but an environment where I could hear God speak.

Do you remember a few weeks ago when we talked about the O.P.R.A. method—where someone points to a random passage in Scripture and tries to figure out how to apply it? The problem with something like that is that reading random Scriptures will not provide solid biblical growth.

One of the ways I encourage people to begin reading the Word for themselves in a way that will fill them spiritually is to read 2 Timothy every day for a week. It is only four chapters long and can be read in one sitting fairly quickly. If you read it every day for a week, you will have read an entire book of the Bible seven times through!

After reading it repeatedly, you will find yourself picking up on words you might have passed over before. Images will come to life. Truths will jump out at you with immediate application.

Be honest—how do you feel when you're reading the Bible?

What are some other short books (besides 2 Timothy) that you could read through in one sitting?

But just reading through a book doesn't address the heart of the issue—Hearing God speak through His Word. It's a great first step, but we have to do like the Israelites did with the manna and make the effort to gather our nourishment for the day.

CREATING AN ATMOSPHERE TO H.E.A.R. GOD SPEAK

If we want the Word to take root in our lives, we need to approach it in a way that we are listening for the voice of God through it. The H.E.A.R. journaling method is an incredibly simple way to do exactly that.

The acronym H.E.A.R. stands for Highlight, Explain, Apply, Respond. Each of these four steps contributes to creating an atmosphere for hearing God speak. Let's see how it works and see it in practice all at the same time.

Let's assume that you begin your quiet time with the book of 2 Timothy, like in our example a moment ago. Before reading the text, pause and sincerely ask God to speak to you. It may seem trite, but it is crucial that we seek God's guidance in order to understand what He wants us to hear in His Word.

Next, in a journal, write the letter "H" in the top-left corner of a blank page. After reading a passage of Scripture, highlight each verse that speaks to you by copying it under the letter "H".

After you have highlighted a passage you want to focus on, write the letter "E" under that entry. Now we begin doing some of the things we learned about in Session 3—we're going to investigate the passage a little bit. By asking some simple questions, we can understand a little bit about what the passage is saying and begin to explain what it means. Why was it written? To whom was it originally written? How does it fit with the verses surrounding it?

After writing a short summary of what you think the text means, write the letter "A" underneath it. This is where we attempt to move from head knowledge to heart transformation, because we are going to discover how these truths apply to us personally.

Like we saw in Session 3, ask some questions to apply the text to your context. How can this help me? What does this mean for me today? If I applied the truths in this verse, how would it look in my life?

Finally, below those three entries, write the letter "R" for Respond. Your response may be a call to action: "Because I read this, I am going to _____." It might be a prayer of thanksgiving. It might be noticing an attitude that you need to change. This is a response to God from the reading of His Word, so it can be as personal as you want to make it.

> *How do you think creating a H.E.A.R. journal could transform your reading of the Word?*

> *What are some struggles you think you might face writing out H.E.A.R. journals?*

This week during your devotions, you will practice writing H.E.A.R. journals. I will provide a sample one for you so that you can see how they look, but remember the point: You want to hear what God is speaking to you through His Word. As you learn how to read it and apply it, you will find that it begins to dwell in you richly and will give you the strength and nourishment you need to live each day as He would have you to.

SAMPLE H.E.A.R. JOURNAL

H (Highlight): "I am able to do all things through Him who strengthens me." Philippians 4:13

E (Explain): Paul was telling the church at Philippi that he has discovered the secret of contentment. No matter the situation in Paul's life, he realized that Christ was all he needed, and Christ was the one who strengthened him to persevere through difficult times.

A (Apply): In my life, I will experience many ups and downs. My contentment is not found in circumstances. Rather, it is based on my relationship with Jesus Christ. Only Jesus gives me the strength I need to be content in every circumstance of life.

R (Respond): Lord Jesus, please help me as I strive to be content in You. Through Your strength, I can make it through any situation I must face.

PRACTICE H.E.A.R. JOURNAL 1

Read Psalm 119:1-18 three times.

Highlight a verse that sticks out to you:

Explain what it means in the context of the passage:

Apply a truth from it to your life:

Respond to God with a prayer, an action, or thanksgiving:

S.7 DAY TWO

PRACTICE H.E.A.R. JOURNAL 2

Read James 1:1-27 three times.

Highlight a verse that sticks out to you:

Explain what it means in the context of the passage:

Apply a truth from it to your life:

Respond to God with a prayer, an action, or thanksgiving:

PRACTICE H.E.A.R. JOURNAL 3

Read 1 John 5 three times.

Highlight a verse that sticks out to you:

Explain what it means in the context of the passage:

Apply a truth from it to your life:

Respond to God with a prayer, an action, or thanksgiving:

PRACTICE H.E.A.R. JOURNAL 4

Read 2 Peter 1 three times.

Highlight a verse that sticks out to you:

Explain what it means in the context of the passage:

Apply a truth from it to your life:

Respond to God with a prayer, an action, or thanksgiving:

MOVING
FORWARD

HAVE YOU EVER THOUGHT ABOUT WHAT HAPPENS to the characters in a movie after the credits roll? I realize they are fictional, but bear with me for a moment.

Think about the kids in the movie *The Goonies*. They find a treasure map, go on a hunt for One-Eyed Willie's treasure, encounter all kinds of adventure and peril, and escape from the most dangerous and thrilling situation of their lives—all before they are old enough to drive. The ending of the movie is triumphant and uplifting, but after the credits roll those kids' lives would quickly go downhill. What on earth could possibly live up to the adventure they had when they were twelve?

They'll eventually have to go off to college, get jobs, and start families—all knowing that nothing life throws at them could ever possibly live up to the life-changing adventure they had when they were barely even teenagers. They had a great time and it was a wonderful story, but whatever comes after their adventures will pale in comparison. See, those kids had a life-changing experience early on, but that experience is hardly the end of the journey set before them. The real adventure of their lives is about to begin—the struggle of living a normal life after having experienced the truly extraordinary.

This is a silly example, but it has a point: One phenomenal experience may be the ending to a Hollywood movie, but it is merely the beginning of what surely comes after it. Discipleship is the exact same way. Meeting and having your life changed by Jesus Christ is nothing short of miraculous and is to be celebrated with great joy—but having your life changed by Jesus is not the end of your story. Discipleship is a lifelong process that merely begins at salvation.

Can you think of any other book or film characters who have a harder journey ahead after having experienced what they did in the famous stories about them?

Have you ever experienced anything truly extraordinary that made other things look dim by comparison?

THE BEGINNING STARTS NOW

I would imagine that first century believers looking at the apostle Paul assumed he had it all figured out. He'd experienced truly remarkable transformation, survived shipwrecks and stoning attempts, and had planted churches all across Europe and Asia. The famous Christian-murderer didn't just have his life changed, but his very name. I would imagine that many Christians thought he'd arrived!

Look at what he tells the church at Philippi, though:

> Not that I have already reached the goal or am already perfect, but I make every effort to take hold of it because I also have been taken hold of by Christ Jesus. Brothers and sisters, I do not consider myself to have taken hold of it. But one thing I do: Forgetting what is behind and reaching forward to what is ahead, I pursue as my goal the prize promised by God's heavenly call in Christ Jesus (Phil. 3:12-14).

Paul argued the complete opposite. He wrote letters that make up a huge portion of the New Testament, made passionate and brilliant defenses for Christian faith, and is considered one of the most influential Christians of all time. But still He declared that he hadn't reached his goal.

Remember, as citizens of heaven, we don't find our success in earthly things, but in heavenly ones. We don't measure our success by how many people were saved because of us, but by how faithful we were to run the race set before us. That means that our goal shouldn't be to make it in the Christian life, but to faithfully carry out the commands that Jesus gave us.

This should not be a disappointing piece of news; it should be the most exciting thing you've ever heard. You have been made into a new creation, given a new purpose, and have access to the limitless wisdom of God Almighty through the Holy Spirit that will allow you to live exactly the life that God designed you to live—one in constant community with Him.

We will never run out of things to learn about God, we will never stop finding new ways to love our neighbors the way Christ did, we will always have more opportunities to share the best news that has ever happened with as many people as we can, and these are all encouraging things.

But best of all, this is not the end of our story, because when we are done on earth, we will return to the kingdom where our citizenship resides—in heaven. Paul recognized this perhaps better than anyone. He knew not to look back to "what is behind" and instead press forward for what is ahead, because it's better than even the greatest things we have experienced in our past.

WHAT NOW?

You've spent almost two months learning about the process of discipleship, but now you get to take what you've learned and live it out. You get to live a life growing C.L.O.S.E.R. to God than ever before, and you get to do as Jesus commanded and teach what you've learned from Him to others—who will then teach others.

You may have had a leader guiding you through the pages of this book, but now we've come to the end of it. As we've discovered, though, the end of this book is not the end of the discipleship process—and now you have a resource that you can use to help someone else begin. Perhaps the next step on your journey is to pray about two or three others that you'd like to take back through this book; you may have people in your life who want to grow C.L.O.S.E.R. to God, but don't know how. What if it's your next step to teach them?

I am going to issue you a challenge that I think you're up for. Pray over the names of two or three people you will ask to do exactly what I just said. Ask them, "Do you want to meet up once a week to read a book with me and learn how to grow closer to God?" Have each of the people you ask read one session a week and then meet up to discuss it. Do this for eight weeks (one week per session) and then make them an offer.

Tell them that you can continue meeting together for about a year. Spend the rest of your year reading through Scripture, memorizing it, writing H.E.A.R. journals, and keeping one another accountable. Then, at the end of that year, pray about finding new people to begin the process over with.

By doing this, you will not only grow more into the image of Christ, but you will establish a habit that will last you a lifetime. Most importantly, you will demonstrate that you have been faithful to the final, great commission of our Savior: to make disciples of all nations.

That, after all, is what we were built to do.

> *Why is discipleship worth doing?*

> *Who am I going to embark on this journey with?*

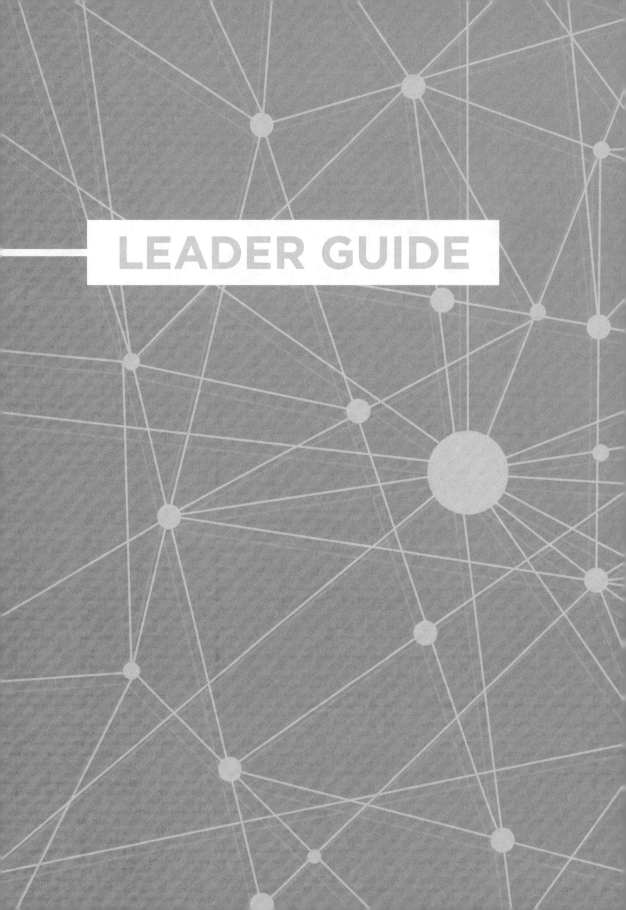

LEADER GUIDE

IN MY YEARS OF DISCIPLING OTHERS, I've found that a group of three to five is the most effective model for investing in others. Jesus demonstrated the benefits of a group of this size with Peter, James, and John. The size is big enough to avoid a one-on-one counseling session, but small enough to encourage *transparency* and *accountability.* Because these elements are essential to spiritual growth, gender specific, closed groups are recommended for confidentiality.

Ideally, D-Groups should meet for 12 to 18 months with the purpose of reproducing after that time. Each member then replicates what was taught to him or her with others. We will experience multiplication in our ministry context similar to what happened in the first century through the disciples.

As your group grows closer together and closer to Jesus through the study and memorization of God's Word, prayer and communication with Him, and practicing the spiritual disciplines, you will be amazed at just how life-changing discipleship can be.

R. Gallaty

Main Objective: To get to know one another by sharing personal testimonies and to introduce the concept of discipleship.

Optional Icebreaker: Go around the room and answer this question: "Of all the things you're involved in, what would you most like to be remembered by?"

Outline:

- Every believer has a testimony.

- Getting "saved" is not the end of your story; it is the beginning.

- Intentionally growing in your relationship with Christ is best done through discipleship.

Prayer prompt: Have each member of your group pray for the person on their right, that they would see the coming weeks as opportunities to grow closer to Jesus.

Follow-up Suggestions: Since it is the first week, follow up with your group members to encourage them to do each of the four personal devotionals, and to come ready to discuss Session 2 next week.

Notes:

Main Objective: To introduce the importance of prayer in a believer's life, to explain what prayer should look like, and to discover just what prayer is.

Key Scripture Reference: Luke 11:1-4

Optional Icebreaker: What is the best way for someone to show you that they care about you? Is it to spend time with you? Buy you things? Tell you words of affirmation?

Outline:

- The only recorded instance of the disciples asking Jesus for specific instruction is when they asked Him to teach them how to pray.

- The "Lord's Prayer" is a six-part "how-to" on how to pray:

  - **Praise:** Our Father in heaven

  - **Purpose:** Your will be done, on earth as it is in heaven

  - **Provision:** Give us our daily bread

  - **Pardon:** Forgive us our debts

  - **Protection:** Lead us not into temptation, deliver us from evil

  - **Praise (again):** Yours is the kingdom and the power and the glory forever

Prayer prompt: Pray for the perseverance to do what it takes this week to develop a consistent prayer life, so that you can each grow closer to God.

Follow-up Suggestions: Throughout the week, give your group updates as to how your prayer life has improved (or even if it hasn't). Your transparency will encourage them to be transparent, too.

Notes:

Main Objective: To discover how to mine God's Word for the truth that He wants us to hear, not for what meaning we want to impart onto it.

Key Scripture Reference: 1 Corinthians 2:12-14

Optional Icebreaker: Use the "O.P.R.A." illustration from the introduction as an activity—take turns opening to random passages and trying to apply them (in as hilarious a way as you can imagine).

Outline:

- The three simple steps to actively reading God's Word:

- Observation—What does the text say?

- Explanation—What does the text mean?

- Application—How does the text apply to me?

Prayer prompt: Pray that as you are faithful to open God's Word this week, He will make His truth clear to you.

Follow-up Suggestions: Throughout the week, periodically check in with your group and ask them what things they're learning from the passages they're studying in their devotions.

Notes:

Main Objective: To understand the important relationship between knowing, loving, and obeying what Jesus says. The more we know Jesus, the more we will love Him. The more we love Him, the more we'll want to obey Him. The more we obey Him, the more He will reveal Himself to us, helping us know Him better.

Key Scripture Reference: 1 John 2:3-6

Optional Icebreaker: How many of the passages you read during the week last week were ones you'd heard of? How did reading them with a new method change your understanding of them?

Outline:

- We love because Jesus loved us first.

- The ultimate display of love is the gospel, which has four main parts:

    - God, the perfect Creator

    - Man, the sinner

    - Christ, the Savior

    - Our response to that knowledge

Prayer prompt: Spend time in personal, private prayer, asking each member of your group to examine their hearts regarding their reception of and belief in the gospel.

Follow-up Suggestions: Throughout the week, ask students how God is asking them to obey Him.

Notes:

Main Objective: Memorizing Scripture is not just a tedious exercise, it's actually a weapon that we can use against sin and temptation.

Key Scripture Reference: Psalm 119:11; Joshua 1:8

Optional Icebreaker: The exercise at the beginning of the lesson deals with movie quotes, so get your students in the "movie mindset" by asking them their favorite movie and then defending their choice against those with differing opinions.

Outline:

- Memorizing God's Word is crucial for a believer.

- We memorize so that we're able to "meditate on God's Word" throughout our day.

- Memorizing God's Word will pay off with tremendous benefits in your spiritual walk.

Prayer prompt: Ask God to help you focus on His Word without distractions, so that you can hide it in your heart and reflect on it throughout your day.

Follow-up Suggestions: Remind students to be working on memorizing Psalm 1:1-2 this week. You'll be asking them to recite it at the beginning of the next session.

Notes:

Main Objective: We don't share the gospel so that we can make ourselves feel better or look super-spiritual; the entire point of sharing God's story is to bring God glory.

Key Scripture Reference: Matthew 28:18-20

Optional Icebreaker: Go around the room and quote Psalm 1:1-2 to each other. If someone is struggling, help them gently and compassionately as a group.

Outline:

- The Great Commission is like the mission we've been sent out into battle with.

- We are to share the good news of Jesus and make disciples of the nations.

- We don't "evangelize" to check a spiritual box or make ourselves feel good; the only outcome we intend to reach is bringing glory to God.

Prayer prompt: Ask students to take a few minutes to analyze their daily actions and their motivation behind those actions. Is the overarching aim of their life to bring glory to God? Pray for God's desires to replace yours, so that you can bring Him the most glory possible.

Follow-up Suggestions: Ask students if God is bringing anyone to mind that needs prayer this week. Take a little bit of time during the week to pray for these people with them.

Notes:

Main Objective: To learn the H.E.A.R. method for journaling so that God's Word will speak loudly and clearly to us as we study it.

Key Scripture Reference: Exodus 16:4-5

Optional Icebreaker: As we begin, Robby explains that he used to get in trouble with his parents when he wouldn't listen to what they were saying. Ask students, "When was a time you got in trouble with your parents?"

Outline:

- **Highlight:** Copy down a verse from your reading that spoke to you.

- **Explain:** Tell what the author was intending to communicate with this verse.

- **Apply:** Describe how the truth from this text can apply to your life today.

- **Respond:** Write out an action or a prayer in response to what God's Word taught you today.

Prayer prompt: Ask students what struggles they foresee when they think of journaling the Bible. Take time at the end to pray for those struggles.

Follow-up Suggestions: Share your H.E.A.R. journals for the week with the people in your group and encourage them to do the same.

Notes:

Main Objective: To take what was learned in this study and replicate it with others.

Key Scripture Reference: Philippians 3:12-14

Optional Icebreaker: What is one thing that you've learned during these eight weeks that you think someone else could benefit from?

Outline:

- As citizens of heaven, we don't find our success in earthly things, but in heavenly ones.

- You've spent almost two months learning about discipleship and growing C.L.O.S.E.R. to God.

- Now it is up to you to continue what you just learned with others.

Prayer prompt: Go around the room and ask if there are any people God is laying on group members' hearts to replicate this process with. Spend time praying for those people specifically.

Follow-up Suggestions: Ask those who are starting groups what you can do to help them. Check in with them periodically in the coming weeks.

Notes:

HOW TO PRAY FOR
LOST FRIENDS AND FAMILY

The purpose of the disciple-making is to help believers grow in their faith and become more like Christ. As we become more like Him, we will be burdened for our lost friends and family and will desire to see them come to know Christ in a more intimate way.

E. M. Bounds wisely said, "You can't rightly talk to men about God until you first talk to God about men." What this means is that our efforts to share the gospel must begin with and be saturated in prayer. Before we can even consider sharing the truth of God with someone who does not believe, we must be covering them with prayer first.

Pray that:

1. God would open their eyes to the truth of the gospel.

> *When anyone hears the word about the kingdom and doesn't understand it, the evil one comes and snatches away what was sown in his heart."* (Matt. 13:19)

> *"In their case, the god of this age has blinded the minds of the unbelievers to keep them from seeing the light of the gospel of the glory of Christ, who is the image of God."* (2 Cor. 4:4)

Satan will do everything he can to blind unbelievers to the gospel. Pray that God would open their spiritual eyes to see the truth.

2. They would seek to know God.

> *"He did this so they might seek God, and perhaps they might reach out and find him, though he is not far from each one of us."* (Acts 17:27)

God will reveal Himself to those who seek after Him. Pray that your lost friends and family would have a hunger for God.

3. They would believe the Scriptures.

Someone who does not know Christ will not understand the truth of the Word.

> *"But the person without the Spirit does not receive what comes from God's Spirit, because it is foolishness to him; he is not able to understand it since it is evaluated spiritually." (1 Cor. 2:14)*

> *"For the word of the cross is foolishness to those who are perishing, but it is the power of God to us who are being saved." (1 Cor. 1:18)*

Pray that they would have a hunger for the Word of God and that they would believe the truths of the Scriptures.

4. God draws them to Himself.

> *"No one can come to me unless the Father who sent me draws him, and I will raise him up on the last day." (John 6:44)*

We must always remember that, although God uses us as the instruments to share the message and help lead people to Him, only He can convict and convert them. One cannot receive Christ until God first draws them. Let us therefore pray that God will draw them to Himself.

5. The Holy Spirit works in their lives.

> *"When he comes, he will convict the world about sin, righteousness, and judgment." (John 16:8)*

> *"When the Spirit of truth comes, he will guide you into all the truth. For he will not speak on his own, but he will speak whatever he hears. He will also declare to you what is to come." (John 16:13)*

Pray that the Holy Spirit will convict them of sin and cause them to repent and believe.

6. God would send someone to lead them to Christ.

> Then he said to his disciples, "The harvest is abundant, but the workers are few. Therefore, pray to the Lord of the harvest to send out workers into his harvest." (Matt. 9:37-38)

Perhaps that someone is you. Pray that you or someone else could be used to show and share the gospel.

7. They confess Christ as Savior and Lord.

> If you confess with your mouth, "Jesus is Lord," and believe in your heart that God raised him from the dead, you will be saved. One believes with the heart, resulting in righteousness, and one confesses with the mouth, resulting in salvation." (Rom. 10:9-10)

> "But to all who did receive him, he gave them the right to be children of God, to those who believe in his name, who were born, not of natural descent, or of the will of the flesh, or of the will of man, but of God." (John 1:12-13)

Pray that they would trust Christ, and confess Him as Savior and Lord!

WEEKEND RETREAT OPTION

A great option to introduce this discipleship strategy to students is through a weekend retreat. Use this simple template to break up the chapter content and build out a meaningful experience for groups.

Friday Night:

Sessions 1-2

Choose questions from sessions 1 and 2 that best fit your group.

Saturday Morning:

Sessions 3-4

Choose questions from sessions 3 and 4 that best fit your group.

Saturday Night:

Sessions 5-6

Choose questions from sessions 5 and 6 that best fit your group.

Sunday Morning:

Sessions 7-8

Choose questions from sessions 7 and 8 that best fit your group.

NOTES